S0-AGF-246

In the
Craftsman
Style

In the Craftsman Style

Building Furniture Inspired by the Arts & Crafts Tradition

The Taunton Press

Publisher: Jim Childs

Associate Publisher: Helen Albert

Associate Editor: Jennifer Renjilian

Editorial Assistant: Meredith DeSousa

Copy Editor: Andrew Delohery

Indexer: Harriet Hodges

Designer and Layout Artist: Susan Fazekas

Taunton
BOOKS & VIDEOS
for fellow enthusiasts

Text © 2001 by The Taunton Press, Inc.

All rights reserved.

Printed in the United States of America

10 9 8 7 6 5 4 3 2 1

The Taunton Press, Inc., 63 South Main Street, PO Box 5506, Newtown, CT 06470-5506
e-mail: tp@taunton.com

Distributed by Publishers Group West

Library of Congress Cataloging-in-Publication Data

In the craftsman style : building furniture inspired by the Arts and Crafts tradition.
       p. cm.
    ISBN 1-56158-398-7
     1. Furniture making. 2. Woodwork. 3. Arts and crafts movement. I. Taunton Press.
TT194 .I5 2001
684.1'04—dc21

00-061512

■ **About Your Safety:** Working with wood is inherently dangerous. Using hand or power tools improperly or ignoring safety practices can lead to permanent injury or even death. Don't try to perform operations you learn about here (or elsewhere) unless you're certain they are safe for you. If something about an operation doesn't feel right, don't do it. Look for another way. We want you to enjoy the craft, so please keep safety foremost in your mind whenever you're in the shop.

In the beginning, there was no thought of creating a new style, only a recognition of the fact that we should have in our homes something better suited to our needs and more expressive of our character as a people than imitations of the traditional styles, and a conviction that the best way to get something better was to go directly back to plain principles of construction and apply them to the making of simple, strong, comfortable furniture.

—Gustav Stickley

CONTENTS

INTRODUCTION

Craftsman furniture is one of the most popular styles with today's furniture makers. In fact, the Arts and Crafts work of hobbyist woodworkers and small-shop professionals through the latter half of the 20th century has probably been one of the reasons for the renewed popularity of the style in the mass-production furniture industry and among today's consumers.

I suspect there are many reasons for this enduring popularity among the cabinetmakers who labor alone in their small garage and basement shops. The style has a friendliness, honesty, and adaptability not found in other furniture. By friendliness, I mean it works in almost any home and beside many other types of furniture. Its honesty comes through in its mostly straight lines, in its sparsity of unnecessary ornamentation, and in its visible joinery. The turn-of-the-century artisans who first popularized the style wanted their hearty construction to be celebrated as a sort of decoration rather than gussying up their pieces with superfluous adornment. The style's adaptability, which today releases most furniture makers to interpret and add or subtract elements freely, has been in the blood of Arts and Crafts furniture since the beginning. There was no workbook that dictated the style's details. Each practitioner 100 years ago seemed to have had a slightly different idea of what Arts and Crafts meant.

This adaptability is reflected even in the names used to refer to the furniture that falls under the umbrella of "Arts and Crafts": Craftsman, Mission, Greene and Greene, or Stickley. The book you now hold in your hands has been assembled from the pages of two Taunton Press magazines: *Home Furniture* and *Fine Woodworking*. The book's editors have assembled—and redesigned—articles about the origins and hallmarks of the Arts and Crafts style (Part One), as well as techniques unique to this furniture and some projects to help you make your own Arts and Crafts pieces (Part Two). Part Three contains a series of photographs with short explanations of inspiring Arts and Crafts work made by some of the best woodworkers now practicing the craft. Together, the sections of the book offer an indispensable guide to this enduring and popular furniture style.

—Tim Schreiner, editor of *Fine Woodworking* and former editor of *Home Furniture*

Style & Design

Begun in response to the Industrial Age, the Craftsman style espoused fine craftsmanship and attention to detail. The origins of the movement still influence those designing furniture today. Indeed, there has been a rebirth of the Craftsman style and its tenets. But the Craftsman style is more of a philosophy than one true style. In fact, many makers created their own unique visions within this style. Here you'll find out about some of the most famous makers and their hallmark designs. You'll also learn about designing Craftsman furniture so you can go beyond the historical examples.

ANNETTE CARRUTHERS

Origins of Arts and Crafts

DESIGN GUIDED BY THE CRAFTSMAN'S HAND. With its exposed joinery and solid stance, Sidney Barnsley's oak buffet from 1897 displays a reliance on the forms of Gothic furniture typical of English Arts and Crafts.

Ninety years after it first swept across the United States, American Arts and Crafts furniture is in a revival that shows no sign of weakening. Entire magazines and books, as well as the work of hundreds of furniture makers, are devoted to the style that has come to be known in its various forms as Craftsman, Mission, Greene and Greene, Arts and Crafts or Stickley furniture. The furniture is so prevalent and powerful that it has come to seem distinctly American. But the ideas and forms of Arts and Crafts were born and bred in England and made their way to America later, in the notebooks of designers who visited there.

The Arts and Crafts Movement in England was a rebellion against the Victorian fashion for dark and frilly interiors. Designers instead made sturdy furniture in simple forms and natural colors, sometimes decorated but often extremely plain. The roughness and simplicity of the work was often shocking. One reviewer in 1899 referred to an Arts and Crafts piece as looking "like the work of a savage." Another reviewer remarked that "the educated man rebels at the idea of being treated as a glorified peasant." Clearly, they had struck a nerve.

But the Arts and Crafts Movement was a rebellion of substance as well as style. Much of its power came from the conviction that art and craft could change society and that the increasingly urban and industrialized society needed changing.

Nearly all English Arts and Crafts furniture demonstrates sensitivity to materials, a taste for simple, often rectilinear forms and a concern for function. But because the goals of the movement were so encompassing, its direction was somewhat diffuse, and the furniture varied in a rather bewildering way. It could be veneered or built in solid wood; it could be fashioned from plain, unpolished oak or exotic ebony, richly inlaid

ARTS AND CRAFTS COTTAGE.
Many English Arts and Crafts designers moved to the country. Edward Barnsley, a second-generation Arts and Crafts furniture maker, lived in this cottage and worked in the attached shop.

with silver and mother-of-pearl. Some makers worked entirely by hand while others used machines. Some designers felt it was essential to be personally involved in the making, and others subcontracted the fabrication or even designed for production.

As the photos on these pages illustrate, despite the common threads running through it, English Arts and Crafts furniture was far from homogeneous. Its legacy to makers in America and Europe lay more in presenting a range of new possibilities than in developing a rigidly defined style.

THE MAN BEHIND THE MOVEMENT

William Morris was the founding spirit of the Arts and Crafts Movement. Best known today for his genius as a pattern designer, Morris was admired by his contemporaries as a poet, craftsman, business entrepreneur, defender of ancient buildings and campaigning socialist. The enormous energy he poured into writing and lecturing made him one of the most influential thinkers of the last century, and his ideas captivated a generation of young architects and designers.

For Morris, political ideas could not be separated from artistic ones. The major theme of his lectures was the belief that all people should be able to do useful work in pleasant surroundings rather than producing shoddy goods in the squalid factories and garret workshops of 19th-century Britain. His views and his designs drew on an admiration for Gothic art and architecture, whose excellence he attributed to the greater freedom of craftworkers in the Middle Ages.

Morris designed only a few pieces of furniture himself, but his ideas guided the furniture produced by Morris & Company (top photo facing page), the design firm he and some friends opened in London in 1861. Morris' conviction that good design could come only through knowledge of the craft led scores of designers in England and America to pick up hand tools for the first time. Morris and his disciples breathed life into the concept of an independent designer/craftsman, taken for granted by many people who run small woodworking shops today.

His ideal was of furniture made for the "good citizen" (by which he meant everyone), furniture that should be "solid and well made in workmanship" and except for movable objects such as chairs "should be made of timber rather than walking sticks." This appeal for heavy furniture deeply influenced English designers such as Sidney Barnsley (top photo p. 12 and photos p. 13) as well as a whole generation of Americans.

TWO VIEWS OF ARTS AND CRAFTS FURNITURE

Taken as a whole, Morris' blend of art, craft and philosophy was so broad that it could be followed in many different ways. The divergent work of two of the movement's most prominent designers, C. F. A. Voysey and C. R. Ashbee, demonstrates just how differently two men could interpret one message.

THE POWER OF PURITY. Rock solid and devoid of decoration, Sidney Barnsley's table from the 1920s distills William Morris' ideal that most furniture be "made of timber rather than walking sticks."

Voysey's furniture, in solid wood, tends toward the simple lines and purity of materials that characterizes what Americans now know as Craftsman furniture. He generally built in Austrian oak and left the wood plain and unpolished. Voysey relied on subtle detailing such as legs chamfered gradually from square to octagonal. He sometimes used brass strap hinges and pierced panels to add interest to a cabinet or dresser, but the overall forms were generally Shaker-like in their clean simplicity (bottom photo, right). Voysey took to heart Morris' insistence on good craftsmanship, but he didn't get involved with handwork himself. He designed his furniture on paper and let cabinetmakers do the building.

Ashbee was at the opposite extreme. His furniture often was decorated with a rich variety of carving, inlay, marquetry, painting, gilding and metalwork, sometimes applied together on the same piece (photo, p. 10). As with most other Arts and Crafts

A NEW CENTURY'S FURNITURE STARTED HERE.
These and other works by Morris & Co. prepared the way for the Arts and Crafts Movement (above). Morris & Co. rejected Victorian fashion and evinced instead reliance on medieval forms and respect for country crafts.

STARK LINES UNDER ELABORATE HARDWARE.
C. F. A. Voysey's 1899 cabinet is typical of English Arts and Crafts in adding ornament to simple forms. Voysey's work prefigured Craftsman furniture in America.

work, the forms underlying this ornament tended to be elemental and rectilinear, but the decoration often was sinuous, with overtones of Art Nouveau. For Ashbee, running a workshop was of prime importance. He modeled his Guild of Handicraft after medieval craftsmen's guilds with a vision to provide untrained boys with an opportunity to become skilled craftsmen.

Between these extreme interpretations of Morris' message, there were many shades of opinion and practice. The 1890s was a period of experiment and enterprise, during which designers found ways of working that suited themselves.

GIMSON AND THE BARNSLEYS

Ernest Gimson and Sidney and Ernest Barnsley fall somewhere between the radically different views of Voysey and Ashbee. They were deeply affected by Morris but created work and a way of life that was entirely their own. They produced perhaps the most impressive furniture of the English Arts and Crafts Movement, furniture that has had a profound influence on woodworking in the 20th century.

Gimson and the Barnsleys were young architects in London in the 1880s and

A CABINET FROM THE COMMUNITY. C. R. Ashbee's writing cabinet in mahogany and holly was made in 1899 by his Guild of Handicraft, a group of craftsmen who worked communally.

absorbed Morris' ideas about the importance for an architect to have a practical knowledge of crafts. When the design firm Gimson and Sidney Barnsley had helped found went out of business, they decided to become furniture makers. At Morris' suggestion, they moved to the lush and hilly Cotswold countryside 80 miles west of London to set up workshops. Sidney Barnsley's brother, Ernest, joined them, and the three craftsmen are remembered today as the "Cotswold Group."

Apart from a similarity of style derived from working closely as friends, Gimson and the Barnsleys shared an attitude toward craftsmanship that had a profound influence on all their furniture. Their appreciation of the techniques of cabinetmaking is revealed in their use of exposed joints, meticulously worked inlays and handmade

TYING TOWN AND COUNTRY TOGETHER. In his walnut and ebony sideboard of 1915 (above), Ernest Gimson blended the rich materials and proportions of a formal sideboard with the heavy chamfers of farm implements and wagons such as the one at left.

hardware. They adopted methods of construction seen on woodwork from a variety of sources, including fine historic furniture but also architectural woodwork and rural crafts such as wheelwrighting and toolmaking. The chamfered edges that are distinctive of their work were derived from their enthusiasm for traditional farm wagons.

Like other Arts and Crafts designers, Gimson and the Barnsleys looked past the

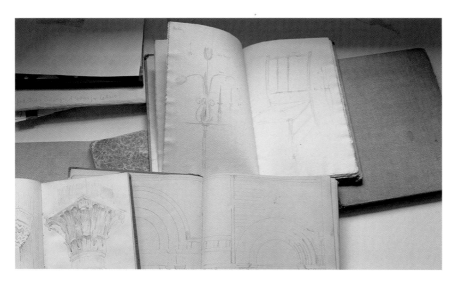

CLASSICAL TRAINING UNDER-
LAY ARTS AND CRAFTS INNO-
VATION. Sidney Barnsley's
sketchbooks teem with render-
ings of buildings, fragments
and furniture from his study
tours of Britain and the
European continent.

because of competition from cheaper and more decorated furniture made in city factories. The influence of country furniture meshed well with Morris' appeal for plain, heavy furniture.

Such simplicity marks much of the work Gimson and the Barnsleys and other English designers produced, but it did not result in the sameness that characterizes much of American Arts and Crafts furniture. In England, a single maker might produce some heavily proportioned pieces in solid wood, with rough country-inspired details and exposed joinery, and other pieces with glossy finishes and complex veneering. The apparent dichotomy can be traced to Morris and his message that furniture fell into two categories, requiring different approaches to design.

One category included "chairs, dining and working tables and the like, the necessary work-a-day furniture." This furniture, Morris felt, should be "simple to the last degree; nay, if it were rough I should like it better." This radical call for roughness from a highly refined designer had a profound impact in America as well as in England.

But Morris thought that people ought to have decorative pieces as well, used sparingly in an interior to provide beauty and focus. He called these pieces "state" furniture: "I mean sideboards, cabinets and the like, which we have quite as much for beauty's sake as for use." On these he suggested that designers spare no ornament and "make them as elegant and elaborate as we can." The impact of this side of Morris' vision is clear in the elaborately detailed casework of Ernest Gimson.

neoclassical furniture that became popular in the 18th century, instead finding inspiration in earlier work. After seeing Gothic pieces in museums and historic houses, they produced coffers and chests made of solid planks as well as elaborately decorated cabinets based on *vargueños,* 16th- and 17th-century Spanish chests on open stands. In farmhouses and inns, they were inspired by settles and buffets by country makers of the 18th and 19th centuries—simple, traditional work that was beginning to die out

A FLAIR FOR THE INFORMAL.
A side chair made in 1891,
before he left London for the
Cotswolds, reveals Ernest
Gimson's affinity for the
straightforward.

Gimson's 1915 sideboard in walnut with an ebony plate rack and understructure (top photo, p. 11) is clearly a piece of state furniture. But in it he deftly blended formal proportions and materials with detailing drawn from country crafts. The carcase of the sideboard sets the formal tone with its bowed center section, custom brass hardware and checkered ebony and holly inlay. On the openwork plate rack and on the legs and the stretchers, however, he employed the heavy

SAVAGE SIMPLICITY. An early bed and chest of drawers by Sidney Barnsley demonstrate the fascination for the forms and details of rough country crafts that led one critic to call his furniture "the work of a savage."

chamfering that he and the Barnsleys had admired on country wagons.

Despite his fascination with the materials and techniques of cabinetmaking, Gimson restricted his hands-on work to making turned chairs while employing others to make his cabinet pieces from his drawings. Like Ashbee, Gimson placed great importance on the training of his craftsmen.

Sidney Barnsley, on the other hand, worked alone for most of his life, enjoying the satisfaction of doing skilled work with his hands. In the chest of drawers he built for his Cotswold cottage (photo, above and right), his love of the craft is written in the directness and the roughness of the piece. He proudly left the dovetails and the tenons exposed and used a simple chip carving pattern to decorate the piece. The chest's pulls, dovetailed into the drawer fronts, are a wonderfully direct and original solution that became a hallmark of his work.

CARRYING ON ARTS AND CRAFTS

By 1916 the Arts and Crafts Movement had burned itself out in Britain as far as the world of art and design was concerned. In America, the movement dimmed at the same time, then went into complete eclipse, reemerging only in the late 1970s as prices for original pieces skyrocketed, and contemporary makers began reproducing and adapting American Arts and Crafts furniture.

In England, however, Arts and Crafts never went away entirely. The work of Gimson and the Barnsleys, in particular, was carried on through the 20th century by a number of furniture makers. After

ONE PART BARN, ONE PART CHAPEL. Ernest Gimson's design for a library at Bedales school reveals his love of the heavy timbers and solid joinery of rural crafts and buildings as well as his training as an architect in a time when the ultimate commission was a church. The chairs were designed by Gimson, the tables by Sidney Barnsley.

ARTS AND CRAFTS EVOLVING. Peter Waals, for many years Ernest Gimson's shop foreman, continued making pieces after Gimson's death in 1919. This Macassar-ebony veneer bookcase (right) from 1937 is based on a Gimson design.

Gimson's death in 1919, his foreman, Peter Waals, continued his work, building slightly altered versions of the master's designs (bottom photo).

Sidney Barnsley's son, Edward, worked from the early 1920s until his death in 1987, making furniture in the Arts and Crafts tradition (bottom photo, facing page) but refined by influences from Regency and Danish design. Many fine craftsmen who have since gone out on their own trained in his shop. The impact of Edward Barnsley's designs and his high standards of craftsmanship is evident in much of the finest furniture being built in America today.

But perhaps the most direct link to the origins of English Arts and Crafts can be

LIVING LINK TO THE ORIGINS OF ARTS AND CRAFTS. Neville Neal has been making chairs to Ernest Gimson's designs for 56 years. He apprenticed with Edward Gardiner, Gimson's chairmaker, and later inherited Gardiner's patterns for all of Gimson's chairs.

found in a small stone building on the main street in Stockton, a tiny country town just north of the Cotswolds. Here, Neville Neal and his son, Lawrence, make chairs to Gimson's designs. Neville Neal was apprenticed to Gimson's chairmaker, Edward Gardiner, in 1939 and has been making Gimson chairs ever since with patterns made from Gimson's original drawings (top photo).

Using wood felled locally and rush they pick themselves, father and son make about 200 chairs a year. Between the two, they have over 80 years of experience. But there is no sense of antiquity in the shop. In their obvious love of the work and in their excellence, the English Arts and Crafts movement is very much alive.

DESIGN FROM FATHER TO SON. Sidney Barnsley's son, Edward, carried on the Arts and Crafts tradition from 1923 until his death in 1987. He made this walnut and ebony bookcase in 1924.

KEVIN P. RODEL

Arts and Crafts Reborn

To an onlooker, making furniture in a period style may seem limiting. But for me it has been liberating. As a self-taught designer, I've found that accepting the restrictions of a period style has helped loose the flow of original design ideas. Rather than doing exact reproductions, I generally design a piece by drawing ideas and elements from a range of pieces and makers. Sometimes I borrow a specific detail, sometimes just a general mood. While many of the ideas are not original with me, there is self-expression in reassembling and reanimating them.

Learning to design this way is a matter of time and experience, just like learning a craft. To become proficient at cutting dovetails, you have to cut a slew of them; every time you cut a set you get a little better, a little faster. With every design done within the parameters of a period style, you learn to use a detail or an element you like, and you can then put it on the shelf and it's yours. The more you master, the more flexible you become in designing.

FINDING THE RIGHT IDIOM

A period style gives you an elaborated structure in which to work. The relationships of details to proportions have already

REANIMATED ARTS AND CRAFTS.
Blending elements from various Arts and Crafts designers, Rodel makes fresh pieces with the feel of the originals. Lamp by Raymond Tillman.

EXECUTIVE ARTS AND CRAFTS. Once mastered, the Arts and Crafts idiom is flexible enough to serve a range of contemporary uses. In his search for the right mood, Rodel doesn't overlook the details, here using an ebony insert to accommodate a lamp cord.

been explored and resolved in thousands of pieces of furniture. These provide a self-guided course in furniture design. But finding the right style for your own work is the necessary first step.

I learned the craft of furniture making—the joinery methods, stock preparation, layout, efficient use of time and materials—by building Queen Anne, Shaker and Federal-style pieces. I learned the styles well enough to make copies, but not well enough to feel entirely comfortable making original pieces in the same mode. Then I began studying

and building Arts and Crafts style pieces, and instantly felt at home. I responded to the visual style and, just as important, to the ideas that spawned it. In Arts and Crafts I found a century-old style that felt entirely current. A major component of the Arts and Crafts philosophy was a belief in the value of craft and craftsmanship. I had staked my career on a similar belief. Because I felt comfortable in its confines, Arts and Crafts enabled me to begin learning the art of design.

ADAPTING, NOT COPYING

I find many Arts and Crafts designs inspiring, but I rarely duplicate them. Some of the chair designs of Frank Lloyd Wright and Charles Rennie Mackintosh, for example, although acclaimed for their beauty, are rated on the opposite end of the comfort scale. Comfort and use are just as important to me as aesthetics. Working the way I do, borrowing here and there, I'm free to adapt a beautiful but uncomfortable or outmoded piece to some new use.

I recently reworked a Mackintosh washstand. The original piece had the proportions, details and mood of a masterpiece. But not many of us have use for a washstand anymore. I was able to keep the overall feel of the original and redesign it as a dining room server (see the photo this page). Since the original was designed to fit snugly into a bedroom alcove, it had very stark sides. I added a carving there in a flower motif that recurs throughout Mackintosh's work. And I replaced a row of cubby holes across the top with a relief-carved panel that gave me a place to install lighting.

So while I look to the past, I design for the present. I make furniture to fit the needs of my customers. Their requirements include space for computers, lighting and compact disc players. I always try to anticipate the compromises such equipment requires by doing little things like accommodating wiring instead of just ignoring it. It's easy to forget, when working out the way a piece will look, that it has to serve a person's needs.

ARTS AND CRAFTS TOOL KIT

You can often recognize Arts and Crafts work by its rectilinearity, exposed joinery and stout construction. But there are a number of other elements I use to evoke the mood of the original work.

Broad, overhanging tops are a familiar statement from the Arts and Crafts period. In my tables and case pieces, an overhanging top is often the dominant horizontal line.

The other less dominant lines take their positions and proportions in reference to it.

Overall, I prefer to emphasize horizontal lines over vertical ones while trying to maintain an interesting interplay between the two. If I can pull it off, I like to "trick" vertical lines into making a horizontal statement. I've done this on the front and sides of the writing desk (bottom photo p. 20) with a row of leather-paneled squares, and in my side chairs, where alternating slats stop short of the crest rail, forming a row of square holes.

MACKINTOSH MODIFIED.
Rodel redesigned the sides and top of a built-in C. R. Mackintosh washstand to make this freestanding server.

INSPIRED BY ARCHITECTURE. The mood and detailing of buildings offer fruitful ideas for furniture. H. H. Richardson's Crane Library (above) inspired Rodel with its powerful presence. Rodel tried to give his desk (below) a similar rootedness with a series of arched forms at the bottom.

my pieces. This is in the tradition of the Arts and Crafts movement, which was as robust in ceramics, glass, fiber and metalwork as in furniture.

Handmade decorative copper, brass and iron hardware are hallmarks of the Arts and Crafts style, and I make use of them frequently. But so are leaded glass, ceramic tiles, leather and inlaid metal or wood. All these materials strengthen the link to the original Arts and Crafts furniture, but they're also a pleasure to use for their own sake. And I enjoy the contact they bring with people working in other crafts.

I often enrich the vertical surfaces of a piece with offsets, shadow lines and piercing to break up broad expanses and to generate a sense of depth. Where vertical and horizontal members meet, I almost always use a shoulder or setback. Breaking up a surface this way creates texture, something more for the eye to explore. To achieve another level of texture, I often incorporate materials from other crafts in

THE INFLUENCE OF ARCHITECTURE

I pay nearly as much attention to the architecture of the Arts and Crafts era as the furniture. Arts and Crafts designers were particularly deliberate about linking the two, but the same correspondence is found in almost all eras.

My large writing desk was directly inspired by buildings. I had seen a side view of Frank Lloyd Wright's Robie House, and

I loved the strong horizontal lines of the roof and the terrace and the way the narrow, vertical windows and intervening mullions formed another strong horizontal band. It struck me as a perfect blend of line and proportion. I was inspired, too, by Wright's Ward Willets house. On the facade of that building I saw a motif of square forms over rectangular ones flanked by broad, vertical piers, which I adopted for my desk. With Wright, although I may derive some detailing from his furniture, I find more ideas in his architecture.

The writing desk is also indebted to the beautiful Romanesque buildings of American architect H. H. Richardson. Although Richardson died in 1886 just as the Arts and Crafts movement was dawning, I find that his massive masonry buildings are quite compatible with the style. The connection isn't in the motifs and details, but in the shared underlying virtues: weight, strength, repose and a nod toward medieval guild craftsmanship.

I've also adopted architectural ideas in a more explicit manner. Sometimes I'll design detailing for a piece of furniture that gives it the feeling of a miniature building. On one glass-front bookcase (see the bottom photo this page) I saw something architectural in the way the posts, back and sides extended above the top. So I added some lines and squares of inlay, giving the piece a castle-like look that solidified the connection.

FINDING THE EXOTIC IN ARTS AND CRAFTS

My small table (photo above right) employs exposed joinery, solid rectilinear forms, and plain native wood. All are basic elements of Arts and Crafts design. But without straying very far, the table also shows how the idiom can be used to express and interpret other ideas.

After making a plainer version, I modified the design to evoke a mood of Moorish architecture. It took just a couple of strokes. First I made a curved cut into the underside of each cross-stretcher. When

these members were assembled, the curves intersected at 90° and created pointed, Moorish arches. I scooped out the bottom of each leg so a very small arch was visible on each face. All these tiny arches around a main central arch were meant to echo the symmetry and clustered arches of a Moorish mosque.

To further suggest this mood, I cut stopped coves (elongated arches) into the bottom edge of the table top. And I added a line inlay around the top. Together, the inlay and the arches create a miniature architectural cornice that I hoped would balance the details in the base and give a slightly exotic flavor to a simple design.

TRANQUIL FURNITURE

One of the fundamental principles of the Arts and Crafts movement is that architecture should not intrude upon the landscape, but be part of it. I've tried to apply the same axiom to furniture, working to design pieces that don't stand out, but become part of the interior landscape. I would prefer that someone entering a room I'd furnished not notice any individual pieces, but instead feel a sense of welcome and tranquility.

MOORISH MISSION. Rodel finds the Arts and Crafts style extremely adaptable. Here he uses a cluster of arches to evoke the design of a Moorish mosque.

FORTIFIED BOOKCASE. Inlaid lines and squares create a scene of miniature battlements surmounting this bookcase.

THOMAS HUGH STANGELAND

Building in the Language of Greene and Greene

I made a roomful of furniture recently in the style of Charles and Henry Greene, brothers who designed houses and furniture in California in the first decades of this century. One of the most difficult aspects of making this furniture was finding ways to produce the details, the little touches that define the Greenes' work and make it so appealing to the hand and eye. The square black pegs, which are left slightly proud of the mahogany surface; the exposed splines also proud and gently radiused back to the surrounding wood; the rounded double-L brackets—these and other signatures of the Greenes' furniture are all deceptively tricky to make well. Once mastered, though, they provide the basic vocabulary for building furniture in the language of Greene and Greene.

SWEET DETAILS DEFINE THE FURNITURE OF GREENE AND GREENE. Learning to produce them is key to making furniture that compares to the originals. The author's sideboard (bottom) and writing desk (top) are fresh designs, but their superbly made and marshalled details give them the ring of the real thing. Both are made of sustained-yield mahogany and Ebon-X, an ebony substitute.

The dining chair in the photo, one of a set of eight I built, is a straight reproduction of a chair designed by the Greenes in 1908. Working from photographs, I followed their example as closely as I could. The only concession the client and I made to cost was to leave out a subtle carving detail at the base of the legs. I took a more interpretive approach when I made the sideboard in the bottom photo (facing page) and the writing table in the inset photo. For each of these, I used a Greene and Greene piece as a starting point but redesigned the original to satisfy the client's needs, the demands of function and my own sense of proportion. (For an account of how the sideboard evolved from its Greene and Greene forefather to my final version, see the story on pp. 26-27.)

SPRINGS OF INSPIRATION

The Greenes' system of detailing did not develop all at once. It grew gradually as they were exposed to a variety of influences and ideas. Like many craftsmen of their day, Greene and Greene were deeply influenced by the Arts-and-Crafts movement. Arising in 19th-century England in reaction to the mechanization and shoddy goods of the industrial revolution, the movement was a call for honest hand craftsmanship. The Greenes were particularly influenced by Gustav Stickley and other proponents of Arts and Crafts who emphasized openly expressed joinery and function before frippery—features also evident in all the Greenes' work.

What sets the Greenes' work apart is the blending of an Oriental aesthetic with Arts and Crafts. In Japanese temple architecture and Chinese furniture, the Greenes saw ways to soften a composition of straight lines and solids by rounding edges and introducing gentle curves. There's an Eastern overtone as well in the balanced but slightly asymmetrical patterns of the Greenes' detailing.

DOING THE DETAILS

It's in the material The impact of the details in the Greenes' furniture is partly a function of the materials they used. Combining ebony and mahogany gives the

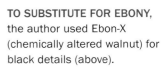

TO SUBSTITUTE FOR EBONY, the author used Ebon-X (chemically altered walnut) for black details (above).

REPRODUCING DETAILS. Square black pegs left proud convey the Greenes' message of hand craftsmanship in the author's reproduction chair (left).

furniture warmth as well as a strong visual contrast. I wanted to achieve the same effects but without using endangered woods. I considered using maple with walnut accents, but I finally chose sustained-yield mahogany and Ebon-X, an ebony substitute made of chemically altered walnut. The chemical treatment gives the Ebon-X a rich black color but also gives it working properties that aren't that far from ebony's.

Square pegs Glinting, square ebony pegs are a hallmark of Greene and Greene furniture. The pegs rise above the mahogany, and each little edge is gently radiused back to the surrounding wood, providing a reflective surface and a tactile message of hand craftsmanship. The pegs emphasize the joints in the furniture and many are caps for counterbored screws. But as I laid out the mortises for them on the crest rails of the chairs, I realized that some of the pegs are purely decorative. I followed the Greenes' example in making the pegs in a variety of sizes, from $\frac{3}{16}$ to $\frac{1}{2}$ in. sq. As far as I could tell, the variation in size was a matter of aesthetics. I found, too, that their placement was not exactly symmetrical. Rather than being lined up in rows, the

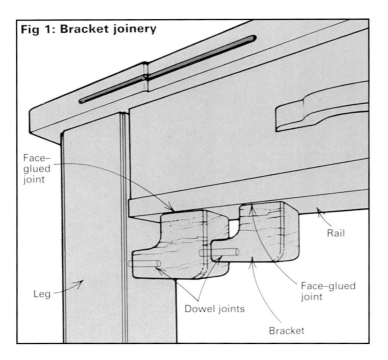

Fig 1: Bracket joinery

Face-glued joint

Leg

Rail

Dowel joints

Face-glued joint

Bracket

CHINESE BRACKETS FOR STRENGTH AND A SINUOUS LINE. Drawn from Chinese furniture, curved brackets (above right) tie Greene and Greene pieces together visually as well as structurally.

BRACKET ALIGNMENT IS TRICKY. At inset right, the author locates a dowel hole on his table by sliding the bracket along a guide board clamped to the apron and marking with a dowel center.

pegs were arranged in subsets slightly offset from each other to add visual interest (see the inset photo, p. 23).

I made ¼-in.-deep mortises for the dozens of pegs with my hollow-chisel mortiser. It makes the job quick; the little tearout is not noticeable after I drive in the slightly oversized pegs. You could also use a drill and chisels or chop the mortises by hand.

To make the pegs, I ripped 8- or 10-in.-long sticks of Ebon-X, so they were exactly square in section and fractionally larger than the corresponding mortises. I squared up both ends of each stick on the disc sander with the stick held against the miter gauge. I sanded out the disc scratches with 150-paper on my hand-held orbital sander. These sanded ends would eventually be the exposed surface of the pegs: achieving a totally smooth surface was essential.

It would be murder to make the tiny radiused edges with the pegs already in their mortises, so I did my shaping ahead of time. I rounded down slightly on each edge at the end of the stick with an orbital sander, keeping the roundovers equal. To get the gleam of polished ebony, I took the sticks to my grinder and burnished the ends with red rouge on a cotton buff wheel.

When I was satisfied with the finish, I bandsawed about ⅜ in. off each end of all the sticks and repeated the process until I had a good supply of pegs. The bandsawn face

would be hidden in the mortise, so I didn't have to clean it up. But I did chamfer the four bottom edges, so they wouldn't hang up or cause tearout when I drove the peg into the mortise. I did the chamfering on my stationary belt sander, holding the little pegs by hand (leave your fingernails a little long for this chore). Or you could do the chamfering against a stationary piece of sandpaper on a flat surface. I put a little glue in the mortise and drove the pegs with a rubber mallet.

Curved brackets Those little double-L brackets below the seat of the chair and the cases of the sideboard and writing table are derived from Chinese furniture. In addition to tying parts together visually and adding a curve, they provide some resistance to racking forces (see the top photo). While they may look innocent, they're quite a challenge to make.

I made the brackets in bunches. I made a Masonite template for each size L and traced it over and over on a board machined to the correct width and thickness. Because the wide end of the L would be face glued, I put it on the edge of the board to give it a long grain surface. I cut the brackets out on the bandsaw and then sanded their outside curves on my stationary disc sander and their inside curves with a sanding drum chucked into my drill press. To be sure I had flat, square glue surfaces, I touched them up using the miter gauge with my stationary disc sander.

All the curved edges on the fronts of the brackets are rounded over, and I did the work with a router inverted in a vise. If you make a

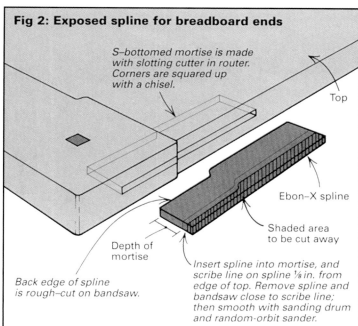

Fig 2: Exposed spline for breadboard ends

S-bottomed mortise is made with slotting cutter in router. Corners are squared up with a chisel.

Top

Ebon-X spline

Shaded area to be cut away

Depth of mortise

Back edge of spline is rough-cut on bandsaw.

Insert spline into mortise, and scribe line on spline ⅛ in. from edge of top. Remove spline and bandsaw close to scribe line; then smooth with sanding drum and random-orbit sander.

small push block with a foam or rubber bottom surface, you'll be able to get your hands away from the action while keeping good pressure on the little workpiece. Because the grain changed direction as I routed around the bend, I found it was important to go fairly quickly and maintain even pressure.

I doweled pairs of L's together and then doweled and face-glued them to the furniture, as shown in figure 1. To drill the dowel holes in the L's, I clamped them in my drill-press vise with stop blocks set up to keep them oriented properly as I tightened the vise.

Gluing up the brackets was a two-stage operation. First I joined the two L's. I laid them on the tablesaw (any reliably flat surface will do) and pushed the dowel joint together by hand. I found if I held them for 30 or 40 seconds, I could leave them and they'd stay tight. When they were dry, I gave them a quick hit on the belt sander to make sure the glue surfaces were flat and square.

The second stage was gluing the brackets in place. To locate the dowel hole in the leg, I put a dowel center in the bracket and slid the bracket along a guide board to mark the spot (see the inset photo, facing page). After I'd drilled the dowel hole, I clamped the bracket in place using one small quick-release clamp to pull the dowel joint tight and another to keep pressure on the face joint.

Exposed splines The arms on the chairs I made are joined to the front legs with large splines shaped in a shallow S. Like the square pegs, the splines are left proud of

the surrounding wood and gently radiused back to meet it. The sinuous black line of the Ebon-X in the mahogany arm emphasizes the joint and underscores its double curve. Here the spline is structural, but where a similar element appears in the breadboard ends of the sideboard and writing table, it is purely decorative.

I made the loose splines for the chair by temporarily screwing a rough-cut dummy spline in the joint and flush-trimming it to the shape of the arm with a router. I removed it and used it as a template with a straight router bit and an oversized bearing wheel to turn out Ebon-X splines ⅛ in. proud of the arm. As with the pegs, I did the sanding, radiusing and burnishing on the exposed edges of the splines before screwing and gluing them in place.

Breadboard on the sideboard I made the tops of my sideboard and desk breadboard style, as the Greenes did. The breadboard ends are decorative in my piece because I used a veneered plywood panel and didn't have to accommodate seasonal movement. The ends are solid mahogany, biscuited and glued to the panel. At the front, I inserted false loose splines of Ebon-X. Because the breadboard ends extend beyond the panel, the splines had to follow in a shallow S-shape, as shown in figure 2 above.

EXPOSED SPLINES MASKED MOVEMENT OF SOLID PANELS IN THE GREENE'S WORK. But the plywood top (above left) won't move. So the spline (above right) is glued to both the panel and breadboard end.

PULLS CAN MAKE OR BREAK A PIECE OF FURNITURE. Experiment to find the right one by mocking up a range of pulls (inset).

With my reproduction Greene and Greene chairs around his dining table, my client asked if I would make a sideboard to go with them. I quickly agreed but soon found it to be an entirely different undertaking. Reproducing the chairs had been a matter of mechanics: I had to figure out how to do what the Greenes had done. But making something in their style to fit a specific site would be a matter of interpretation.

My starting point for the commission was a sideboard the Greenes' made in 1909. But I would have had to contort the original to make it fit the site. The three drawings at right show the development of my sideboard: the Greene's original (top), a drawing midway in the adaptation (center) and the final version (bottom).

SITE SPECIFICS

The client intended the sideboard to be a visual anchor at the end of the room, so it had to be visible above the backs of the dining chairs. And it had to fill a long alcove. These requirements brought the sideboard's overall dimensions to 7 ft. long and 42 in. high—quite a bit longer and higher than a typical sideboard. I would have to do all I could to keep the piece from looking abnormally high.

REAPPORTIONMENT

The Greenes' sideboard has doors at each end and a bank of wide drawers in between. I decided to change this arrangement for several reasons. First, because the sideboard had to be so long, drawers located in the center would wind up being far larger from side to side than they were from front to back: a recipe for drawers that bind. I also thought wide, central drawers would emphasize the length of the piece. And my client, who entertains

on a large scale, was concerned that the cabinets in the original were on the small side. I solved all these problems by moving the doors together into the middle, so they would open on one large cabinet and by splitting the drawers into two banks, one on either

side of the doors, as shown in the center drawing.

To help mask the height of the sideboard, I resorted to unusual proportioning on the drawers. Where a normal silverware drawer is 3 in. high, I made these 6 in. It would have been possible

Evolution of a sideboard

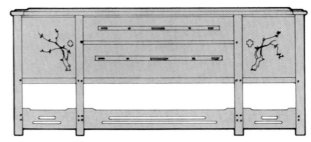

Sketch for Thorsen House sideboard, Greene and Greene, 1909

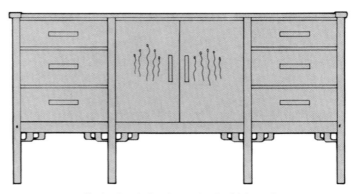

Early sketch for the author's sideboard

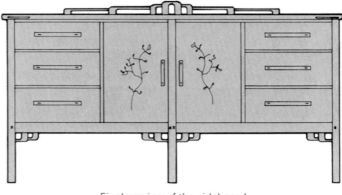

Final version of the sideboard

to stay closer to normal sizes if I had added a fourth drawer, but having more drawers in a stack emphasizes the vertical lines. I also preferred the appearance of three drawers. Call it mystic balance if you will, but an odd number of drawers always looks better to me.

HOW MANY LEGS?

The Greenes' sideboard has eight legs joined by wide stretchers. I decided to omit the stretchers and adopted the bracket detail from the chair to add decoration and a bit more strength below the case. But the number of legs didn't seem right. I did a sketch of a sideboard with four legs, but I thought such a long sideboard would appear ill-supported on four legs even if it could have been made soundly. I drew a version with eight legs (see the center drawing). But that tended to emphasize the height of the piece and made for a clutter of brackets. So I drew a version with six legs; that immediately looked right to me.

PLATE RAIL

With the placement of the legs, doors and drawers determined, I turned to the plate rail. The Greenes' sideboard has a low, solid plate rail. I wanted something that would lighten the sideboard and relate to the brackets, so I designed a low, open plate rail by adapting the bracket shape, stretching it out horizontally. I also took the opportunity to make a visual link to the legs. By creating a little vertical center point in the plate rail, I carried through the line of the middle leg.

I used my bracket-making techniques to produce the parts of the plate rail. I doweled the parts together as before, but because the assembled rail was somewhat delicate, I screwed it to the sideboard's top from below rather than gluing it. This way, I could transport it separately and then attach it on site.

I routed mortises for the splines with a slot-cutter fitted with a bearing wheel. After chiseling out the ends of the mortises, I cut Ebon-X splines to length and rough-cut their back edges to the shallow S-shape on the bandsaw. Like the square pegs, the false splines stand proud of the surface, so I put them in temporarily and scribed a line following the contour on the edge but spaced away ⅛ in. Then I removed the splines, and bandsawed to the line. I gently radiused the edges that would be exposed, sanded and burnished them and glued them in place.

Pulls If a door or a drawer front could be compared to clothing on a person, then knobs and pulls would be like neckties, pins and earrings—finishing touches that are key to the overall impact of a piece. I used the same type of pull on the table drawers as I made for the sideboard. I tried a number of different sizes before settling on the right one for each piece, as shown in the bottom photo. The pulls are a variation on the Asian "cloud lift," an abstract representation of clouds found throughout the Greenes' work. I bandsawed the pulls and filed and sanded to finished shape; then I radiused the edges with a router. I had to scale them down considerably from the ones used on the sideboard. For the sideboard, I decorated them with square pegs, but on the smaller pulls for the writing desk, I found they looked cramped so I left them off.

A fitting finish I wanted the pieces I made to have an immediate presence, a feeling of having been around for a long time: In a sense, they had been. To achieve it, I treated the wood with potassium dichromate, an oxidizing agent borrowed from photographic processing. It comes in powder form and is mixed with water and sponged on. Before applying it, I wet-sanded every surface to raise the grain and knock it back down. While applying the potassium dichromate, I kept an air hose handy to disperse the puddles that formed in the inside corners. If they are left to stand and soak in, the color will be uneven. I then sprayed three coats of catalyzed lacquer, sanding between coats with 320-grit paper.

RENOVATING AN OLD STYLE.
The light and airy, updated
Arts and Crafts furniture of
M. T. Maxwell Furniture Co. fits
well in a contemporary home.

BARBARA MAYER

Thoroughly Modern Morris

Pleasing proportions, beautiful wood and simple lines have made Arts and Crafts furniture a favorite with furniture makers and an informed public. These days, the rest of the world is also taking an interest. The style that stands midway between the uncompromising lines of early modernism and the wild eclecticism of today's art furniture has become popular enough to be featured in the pages of the L. L. Bean catalog and in the showrooms of North Carolina-based production factories as well as in woodworkers' booths at crafts fairs. It goes by several names: Mission, Stickley, Craftsman, as well as the all-encompassing Arts and Crafts.

With so many of the turn-of-the-century originals widely available in antiques shops, today's craftsmen are updating the style by lightening its scale and hue, broadening its design motifs and introducing needed new forms such as computer furniture, oversize beds, coffee tables and electric light fixtures.

SCALING DOWN DIMENSIONS

"The Mission style was always too heavy for me," says Seattle furniture maker Richard LeBlanc. "I wanted a more contemporary look that would work in homes today, so I scaled down the dimensions."

Often, the same individuals who can lovingly reproduce signature pieces by Arts and Crafts masters such as Charles Rennie

THEN AND NOW. The Dirk van Erp lamp, Limbert cutout stand and inlaid Morris chair (top) typify the work done at the turn of the century by America's Arts and Crafts artisans. Today, Green Design Furniture Company has angled and tapered the lines of the traditional Morris chair (lower photo) as well as lightened its finish and upholstery.

■ 29

SOUTHWESTERN MISSION. Today's artisans often keep the simple, straight lines of the Arts and Crafts originals, but add inlay and metal details that give pieces a regional look.

AN ENGLISH ANCESTRY. John Lomas of Vermont's Cotswold Furniture Makers was influenced by the less-rectilinear British Arts and Crafts. His dining table has heavy chamfers and carved decoration.

Mackintosh, Gustav Stickley, C. F. A. Voysey and the Greene brothers are venturing into new territory with adaptations. "After 11 years of reproducing Voysey, I feel I can move off in a slightly different direction," says David Berman, a furniture maker in Plymouth, Massachusetts. He

builds exact copies of furniture by famous English Arts and Crafts-era furniture makers, but also makes his own lamps and light fixtures based on Voysey's design motifs.

The foundations of new Arts and Crafts furniture remain the same: showcased wood grain, beautiful proportions and visible joinery. In general, today's adaptations are showier than the originals, sometimes in subtle ways. For example, some furniture has tapered rather than straight legs; other pieces have contrasting wood inlays and cutouts, or decorative metal hardware that is not authentic but is selected because it looks good with the furniture.

SLENDER LEGS AND LIGHT FINISHES

Although the Arts and Crafts style always offered more variety than is generally recognized now, the scale of the new pieces today tends to be lighter than the most familiar of these designs. A sense of delicacy is achieved by the use of wider overhangs, more slender legs and posts, less figured woods, and lighter finishes.

The changes take many pieces well beyond the realm of strict reproductions. These innovations are being welcomed by the public as invigorating offshoots, not condemned as unwarranted liberties. This acceptance goes against the usual cries of barbarism that accompany attempts to update classic designs.

Modernizers of the Arts and Crafts tradition are faring well partly because they keep to the spirit of the original movement. The best adaptations retain the feeling of simplicity and structural integrity that was present in the originals, and the makers typically reveal an understanding of and love for the earlier pieces. Furthermore, many furniture artisans today are philosophically in the same camp as their forebears.

The Arts and Crafts style originated as a protest against what its devotees saw as "false" values characterized by the overdressed rooms and gimcrack factory furniture of the late 19th century. Some of the style's pioneers also attempted to create fur-

niture in an environment that accorded some independence to workers.

Much of today's Arts and Crafts is being made in very small woodworking shops across the country where the owners share many of these same ideals. "I started out sculpting, carving, using fancy woods, doing bent laminations," says M. T. Maxwell, a furniture maker from Bedford, Virginia. "I got sick of it. I wanted to do something functional, to be able to sell five pieces for the same amount of money as one of the fancier pieces and have people feel good about what they were buying."

USING TECHNOLOGY WHEN IT IS APPROPRIATE

While embracing the values of their predecessors, many Arts and Crafts furniture makers today have no interest in turning back the clock when it comes to technology and materials. The signature Arts and Crafts wood was quartersawn oak with a relatively dark finish, says Peter Smorto, co-owner of Peter Roberts Gallery, a New York City antiques shop for Arts and Crafts originals. Today, the favored wood is cherry, a less coarsely figured hardwood that is typically given a light finish.

"If Gustav Stickley had access to contemporary finishes, I doubt he would have been using ammonia, which is time-consuming, irregular and unpredictable," says Richard Preiss, a furniture maker in Charlotte, North Carolina. Preiss uses modern varnishes that are far more predictable and durable. Even the Stickley company, which promotes its preference for doing things as Leopold and John George Stickley

BUNGALOW BEAUTIFICATION. When today's owners of early 20th-century bungalows remodel their homes, they often fill them with updated versions of the Arts and Crafts furniture that filled them originally.

EAST MEETS ARTS AND CRAFTS. This Tansu china cabinet made by Berkeley Mills blends basic Arts and Crafts through-tenon construction with traditional Japanese drawer handles and doors.

(brothers of Gustav) did, has substituted contemporary pigmented oils and water-based dyes and stains for the ammonia fuming that was popular early in this century. "We put the Stickleys on a pedestal, but they had to get the production out," says William DeBlaay, director of design and product development at today's L. & J. G. Stickley, Inc. "They were running a factory, too. There were bandsaws, mortising machines, and a division of labor."

MAKING FURNITURE FOR TODAY'S WORLD

The craftsmen at Cotswold Furniture Makers in Whiting, Vermont, apply traditional hand-rubbed oil and wax finishes to furniture based on English originals. One of the principals of the company, John Lomas, grew up in the Cotswolds, about 100 miles west of London, where furniture by Ernest Gimson and Sidney and Ernest Barnsley was plentiful. Lomas uses power tools such as a mortiser and a shaper even though the Barnsleys and Gimson disdained the use of anything but hand tools. The methods may have changed, but the Arts and Crafts business philosophy remains. "We make this furniture one piece at a time, with a view to

PACIFIC STYLE. The early 20th-century work of California architects Charles and Henry Greene incorporated Asian details. Today's reproductions, such as this chair and tables by David Hellman, change little from the original.

NEW FORMS. Artisans working today in the style have adapted the original forms to fit in with contemporary needs. New forms include queen-size beds such as this one by Seattle furniture maker Tom Stangeland.

the pieces being in good condition in 200 or 300 years," he says.

In general, however, when today's woodworkers believe that traditional methods yield superior results, they use them. "With most of the Greene and Greene pieces, shaping out of solid material was done by hand," says David Hellman of Watertown, Massachusetts. "There is no machine that can do that. I also stick with a hand-rubbed oil finish, as they would have done."

In addition to using some new technology, today's artisans are adapting the style's forms to today's needs—even those unknown at the beginning of the century—and that is one reason why the furniture is doing so well with consumers. Kevin Rodel adapted Mackintosh's tiled bedroom washstand (now in the collection of the Metropolitan Museum of Art in New York) into a dining room serving piece. Retaining the form and tile treatment, he added more side detailing and changed the top slightly to accommodate recessed lighting.

Furniture makers are using traditional Arts and Crafts details in producing coffee tables, entertainment centers and queen- and

king-size beds—forms that didn't exist 90 years ago. They also are building these new pieces with today's demanding consumer in mind. "Most of our customers like the old look, but they want a sofa or a chair that feels comfortable to them," says Gene Agress, a founder of Berkeley Mills furniture makers in Berkeley, California. "Arts and Crafts seating did not provide all that much lower back support or arm support. People sat on top of the chair, not in it as is preferred today. We had to make the back pillow thicker and the arms on our sofas wider."

A NEW SLANT ON THE STYLE. In updating the Arts and Crafts style, Kevin Kopil Furniture Designs has tapered the legs of its dining table, "floated" the top and put the contrasting ebony slats into groups of threes.

Projects & Techniques

Now that you've learned about the hall-marks of the style, we'll take a look at some creative projects. Whether you want to build a Stickley table, a Craftsman wall cabinet, or a Mission-style mantel, you'll find what you're looking for in this section. At the end of the section, we'll address some techniques common to Craftsman furniture. You can apply these techniques to any of the projects here, or whatever you design on your own.

REX ALEXANDER

Building a Chair, Arts-and-Crafts Style

When the curator of Dennos Museum in Traverse City, Mich., asked me to design and build some Arts-and-Crafts style furniture for an upcoming exhibit, I jumped at the chance. We agreed that I'd look for a customer who would buy the furniture after the exhibit. I approached Jay and Sue Wisniewski, who have been steady clients on a number of projects. They were excited by the idea.

I immediately ordered more than $100 worth of books by or about Stickley (see the further reading box on p. 42), Greene and Greene, Roycroft and others. These books gave me a feel for designs of this period. And they told me what type of wood to use and how it should be cut and finished. I studied detailed drawings and proportions to help with the design.

The deal with the museum didn't work out, but my clients gave me the go ahead for a dining table and some chairs. We still had to agree on a final design, and it had to be compatible with a reproduction Frank

A Stickley Style Dining Chair

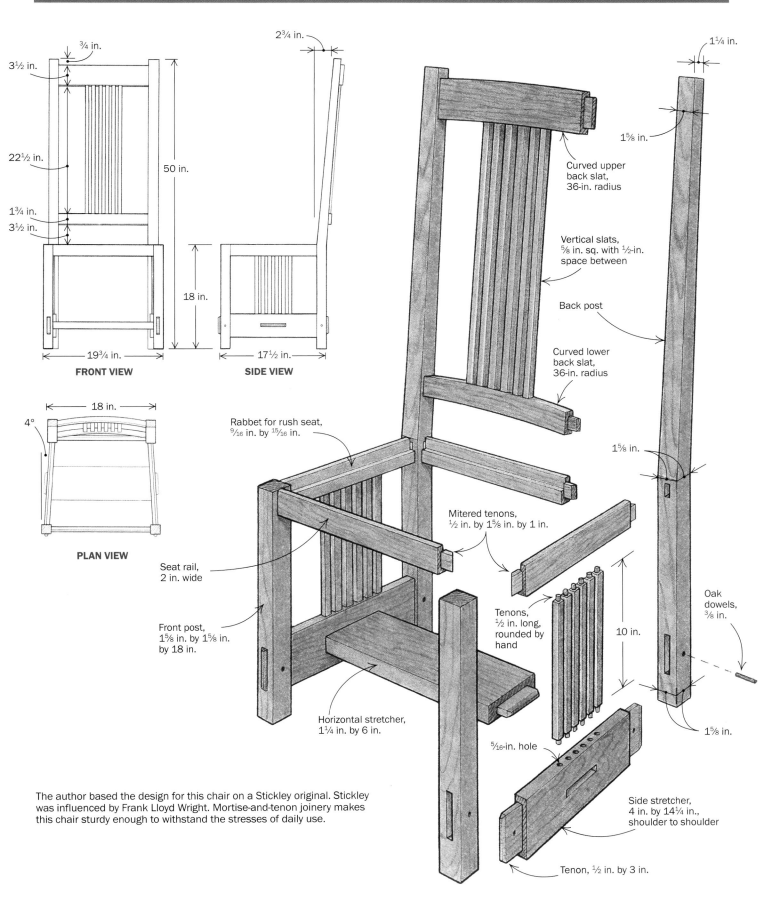

FRONT VIEW

¾ in.

3½ in.

22½ in.

1¾ in.

3½ in.

50 in.

18 in.

19¾ in.

SIDE VIEW

2¾ in.

17½ in.

PLAN VIEW

18 in.

4°

Curved upper back slat, 36-in. radius

Vertical slats, ⅝ in. sq. with ½-in. space between

Back post

Curved lower back slat, 36-in. radius

1¼ in.

1⅝ in.

1⅝ in.

1⅝ in.

1⅝ in.

Rabbet for rush seat, 9/16 in. by 15/16 in.

Mitered tenons, ½ in. by 1⅝ in. by 1 in.

Tenons, ½ in. long, rounded by hand

10 in.

Oak dowels, ⅜ in.

Seat rail, 2 in. wide

Front post, 1⅝ in. by 1⅝ in. by 18 in.

Horizontal stretcher, 1¼ in. by 6 in.

5/16-in. hole

Side stretcher, 4 in. by 14¼ in., shoulder to shoulder

Tenon, ½ in. by 3 in.

The author based the design for this chair on a Stickley original. Stickley was influenced by Frank Lloyd Wright. Mortise-and-tenon joinery makes this chair sturdy enough to withstand the stresses of daily use.

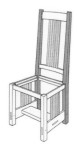

A PLYWOOD JIG FOR SHAPING THE BACK POSTS. A little time invested in this jig guaranteed that all back posts would be the same size and shape. A shaper with a rub collar works as well as a router.

A JIG FOR TRIMMING THE BACK POSTS TO SIZE AND SHAPE
This jig is sized to handle two legs at a time. After cutting the profile for the front of the leg, the author moves the leg to the back of the jig and finishes the profile.

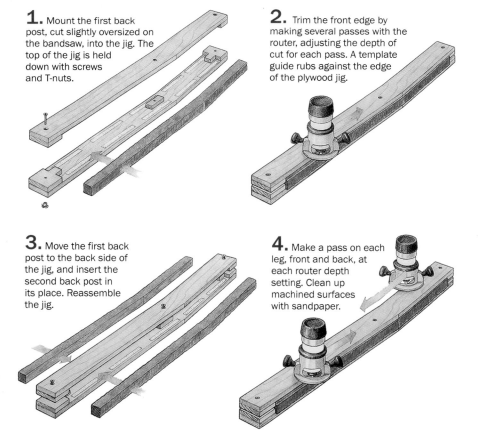

1. Mount the first back post, cut slightly oversized on the bandsaw, into the jig. The top of the jig is held down with screws and T-nuts.

2. Trim the front edge by making several passes with the router, adjusting the depth of cut for each pass. A template guide rubs against the edge of the plywood jig.

3. Move the first back post to the back side of the jig, and insert the second back post in its place. Reassemble the jig.

4. Make a pass on each leg, front and back, at each router depth setting. Clean up machined surfaces with sandpaper.

Lloyd Wright chandelier they had already bought for the dining room.

I learned that Gustav Stickley, in designing his No. 384 chair, was influenced by Wright's work. I knew I had found the inspiration to my design problems. It was this chair (first built in 1905), with its rush seat and vertical slats on both the sides and the back, that I drew upon to arrive at the final design for these chairs. The chairs are shown in the photo on p. 36.

SOLVE PROBLEMS BY BUILDING A PROTOTYPE

I developed a scale drawing of the chair to help determine a materials list (see the drawing on p. 37). For several reasons, I also decided to build a prototype: the joinery is complicated, I had to buy tooling and make jigs, and I wanted to be sure my clients were satisfied with the comfort of this chair. Also, I could use the prototype to verify the proportions and to resolve some of the details of the frame and the fit of the inset rush seat.

Building six chairs is a small production run. A prototype helped me to organize each step and avoid many construction problems. I made the prototype with poplar scraps accumulated from other jobs and assembled it without glue so it could be taken apart. A mistake with poplar at this stage would not be too costly.

Once I was happy with the prototype, I took it apart and measured each piece for a final materials list. Each chair was made from front and back posts, seat rails, side stretchers, a horizontal stretcher, curved upper and lower back slats and vertical slats. There were 35 parts in all, including four oak dowels to pin the stretchers to the front and back posts.

MACHINING THE PARTS

All the parts started out as 8/4 quartersawn white oak. I could resaw the 2-in.-thick material into ⅞-in. seat rails, stretchers, and slats and still have plenty of material for the 1⅝-in.-sq. front and back posts. For a table, six side chairs and two arm chairs, I ordered 400 bd. ft. I wanted heavily rayed pieces for the sides of the front and back posts, the bottom side stretchers and the curved upper and lower back slats. I chose lightly figured white oak for the seat rails.

Except for the back posts, I rough-cut all the chair parts on a tablesaw and then cleaned them up with a jointer and a planer. Later, after making tenons, I cut out the curved upper and lower back slats on the bandsaw (see the top photo on the right), marked with a ¼-in. plywood template made to a 36 in. radius. I cleaned up the bandsaw marks with a spokeshave and a compass plane.

I made a special jig to clean up the back posts after they had been rough-cut to size on the bandsaw (see the photo and drawing at left). The jig is based on one in *Tage Frid Teaches Woodworking: Furnituremaking* (The Taunton Press, 1985).

Two legs are sandwiched between two pieces of birch plywood. One side of the jig is shaped for the outside cut and the other for the inside cut. Support blocks on each end and one in the middle of the jig register the pieces to be cut. Machine screws through one side thread into T-nuts in the other side and hold the legs firmly in place. I applied strips of self-adhesive sandpaper to the inside of each piece of the plywood jig to keep the legs from slipping.

I trimmed the legs to size with a 3-hp router equipped with a ⅝-in. template guide and a 4-in. solid carbide up-cut spiral bit. I cut the front of each leg first and then moved it to the other side of the jig against the registration blocks. You can avoid too much stress on the bit and prevent tearout by making several passes with the router, adjusting the depth of cut a little at a time.

CUTTING THE MORTISES

All the chair parts except for the vertical slats are connected with ½-in. mortise-and-tenon joints. Years ago, I developed a simple jig to cut the mortises for a batch of screen doors, and I was able to use it again for this project (see photos 1-4 on p. 40). This jig is made of ¾-in. plywood with sides that act as a carriage for the router. A ⅝-in. slot runs down the middle of the jig, stopping 2 in. from

■ Cutting curved back slats

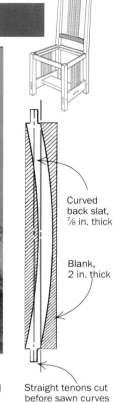

Curved back slat, ⅞ in. thick

Blank, 2 in. thick

Straight tenons cut before sawn curves

CUTTING THE CURVED BACK SLATS. Convex and concave cuts from 8/4 lumber yielded ⅞-in.-thick slats, after the surfaces were scraped clean. These slats are the only curved pieces of the chair.

■ Cutting angled tenons

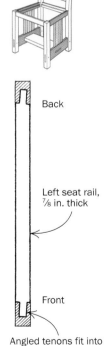

Back

Left seat rail, ⅞ in. thick

Front

Angled tenons fit into straight-cut mortises.

DOUBLE-BLADE TENONING ON THE TABLESAW. With a custom-made jig, the author cut angled tenons for the side stretchers and side seat rails. Sawblades were set at a 4° pitch to the surface of the saw table and separated by a ½-in. spacer.

1. Movable base supports make adjustments easy. Built for mortising a set of doors, this jig can be adjusted to cut mortises in stock of different widths.

2. Use chair part to set jig. After securing one base piece, the author snugs the other one against a side stretcher and screws it in place.

3. Stop blocks for the router determine the length of the mortise cuts and keep them all consistent. Pencil lines help to align the stock.

4. The depth of the mortise is controlled by the plunge mechanism on the router. The author secures stock to the jig with C-clamps.

each end. Two adjustable stop blocks sit square in the carriage and control the length of the mortise.

I held the piece to be mortised in the jig by clamping it to the underside, below the ⅝-in. slot. I used my 3-hp router with a ½-in. by 4-in. solid carbide up-cut spiral bit, adjusting the depth of cut with stops on the router. Even with the jig, this was a time-consuming process.

Router bits don't cut square-cornered mortises. Rather than cleaning out all the corners by hand, I devised a method that works really well. I chucked a Lie-Nielsen corner chisel into my drill press (make sure it's unplugged). I clamped an adjustable fence to the drill-press table to rest the stock against and squared the chisel to the fence. The rack-and-pinion force of the drill press pared a clean, sharp corner in the mortise.

CUT THE TENONS ON THE TABLESAW

All the Stickley chairs that I've seen are wider in front than in back. The side chair in Gustav Stickley's *Making Authentic Craftsman Furniture* narrows toward the back by 1¾ in. I built these chairs to that dimension— 19¾ in. wide at the front and 18 in. wide at the back, with a seat depth of 17½ in. Because of this design detail, either the mortises or the tenons have to be angled on the seat rails and the stretchers. I decided it was easier to angle the tenons. I used the tenoning jig shown in the bottom photo on p. 39.

By drawing the seat-plan view to full size on a scrap of plywood, I determined that the front and back of the chair related to the sides by 4° off square, or 86°, so I set the sawblade to that angle. To cut the cheeks of the tenons on the seat rails and bottom stretchers, I used two blades of a dado set with a ½-in. spacer between them. You can adjust the height of the blades off the table to account for tenons of different length.

After cutting all the angled tenons, I straightened the blade mechanism back to 90° to cut all the cheeks for the horizontal stretcher, front and back seat rails, and the upper and lower back slats. The tenons for all these pieces are straight—parallel to the pieces themselves.

Next I removed one of the dado blades from the table and set the remaining blade at 4° to cut half the shoulders of the angled tenons. I used a miter gauge with a positive stop. I lowered the blade, still set at 4°, and moved the miter gauge to the other slot to make the shoulder cuts on the other side.

Then I straightened the blade and adjusted the height for cutting the shoulders of the

rest of the tenons, except the horizontal stretcher. That piece has straight tenons, but the ends of the piece are cut to 86° to follow the shape of the chair seat. So the shoulder cuts for the horizontal stretcher are cut at 86° with the miter gauge.

The tenons for all the ⅜-in.-sq. vertical slats were simple to make. To get ⁵⁄₁₆-in.-sq. tenons, I cut all four sides at each end with a dado blade. A wooden backer board mounted with double-faced tape held each piece firmly against the miter gauge. I cut each piece slowly to avoid tearout on the corners of the slats. I used a sharp knife to carve the tenons down to a dowel shape to fit ⁵⁄₁₆-in. holes drilled in the back slats, the side stretchers and the seat rails.

FINE-TUNE AND DRY-FIT THE PARTS

Before final assembly with glue, I always like to check the joinery by dry-fitting the parts (see the photo on p. 42). It helps me avoid surprises when I can least afford them. I check the fit of every piece and make adjustments as necessary with a chisel or a shoulder plane.

I marked the through-dowel pins for the lower stretchers (⅜ in. dia.) with a homemade gauge at 4 in. up from the bottom of each post. I drilled halfway in from either side with a Forstner bit in the drill press. Scraping and sanding removed all the milling marks and provided a smooth surface for finishing. After a satisfactory dry-fit, I completely disassembled the chair and stained all the parts.

You have to think through the order in which the pieces of a chair go together, but it's really pretty simple. Vertical slats went in first, glued into both the back slats and the side-stretcher and seat-rail assemblies. I assembled whole sides by adding the front and back posts and clamped them to dry overnight. The next day, I put two sides together with the horizontal stretcher, the front and back seat rails, and the back-slat assembly to make a complete chair frame. I let any glue squeeze-out around the joints cure partially before removing the glue with a sharp chisel.

DRY-ASSEMBLE ALL THE PIECES. This dress rehearsal for the final assembly helps the author avoid the costly mistake of glued joints that don't fit.

After the glue had cured, I removed the clamps and glued and screwed ⅞-in.-thick corner blocks to the inside bottom of the chair. These add stability to the frame and support the inset rush seat. I go over the chair completely with 400-grit wet-or-dry sandpaper and follow that with a good rubdown using #0000 steel wool.

A FINISH FROM SAM MALOOF

Oil on wood is really a beautiful finish, bringing out a depth that looks superior to any film finish. But on furniture and cabinets that come into contact with water, I had been hesitant to use such a finish until I read about Sam Maloof's three-part formula. He mixes equal parts of raw tung oil, boiled linseed oil and polyurethane. The polyurethane prevents this finish from showing water spots.

With the temperature about 50° to 60°F, I sprayed this concoction on the chairs and let it soak in for 10 to 20 minutes. After that, I wiped it off with a rag, using a circular motion. I repeated this procedure two times, letting each coat dry a few days. Then I gave all the surfaces a final buff with #0000 steel wool.

The Maloof technique also calls for another mixture: equal parts tung oil, boiled linseed oil and beeswax. To make this, I melted some beeswax in a double boiler on the stove. While that was still in liquid form, I added the tung and linseed oils, mixing them together. When this mixture cools to a paste, it's easy to apply with a cotton cloth, rubbing in a circular motion. I applied three coats to the chairs. The beeswax gave this finish a nice, satiny glow.

THE FRAME AND FIBER RUSH SEAT

Unlike most chairs made with a rush seat, this one has a separate frame screwed into place after it was woven. Fiber rush exerts a tremendous amount of pressure on a frame, so I decided to use plywood, figuring the multiple alternating layers would hold up better over time. A ¾-in. piece of plywood, cut out in the middle to make a 1½-in.-wide frame, worked best.

To learn how to weave a rush fiber seat, I consulted an article in *Fine Woodworking* #85 (p. 51). As a source book for materials, *The Caner's Handbook* by Bruce W. Miller and Jim Widess came in handy. It is published by Lark Books, 50 College St., Asheville, NC 28801, and it's available from Woodcraft Supply (800) 542-9115 or The Woodworkers' Store (800) 279-4441. The weaving process was time-consuming. Each seat took about a day to complete.

FURTHER READING

Gustav Stickley built many fine examples of Arts-and-Crafts furniture in his factory. He also left a wealth of information in his monthly magazine *The Craftsman* (1901-1916). Much of this information has been republished in two books: *Craftsman Homes: Architecture and Furnishings of the American Arts and Crafts Movement* (available on Amazon.com) and *Making Authentic Craftsman Furniture* (available through Manny's Woodworkers Place, 800-243-0713). Both are published by Dover Publications, 31 E. 2nd St., Mineola, NY 11501. ∎

LARS MIKKELSEN

Coffee Table Is Spare and Sturdy

SIMPLICITY SIMPLIFIED. Lars Mikkelsen picked the functional Craftsman style for this low table and pared it down to its essence.

Ever since I started building furniture, I've taken pleasure in making the many different components in a piece and seeing them all fit together like pieces of a puzzle. As I progressed as a craftsman, the joints got better and more complex, and my enjoyment of the process increased. But making a lot of tight-fitting joints can be quite time-consuming and expensive, and most of my clients have tight budgets. They have come to me because they want something more than they can get in the department store, but they can't necessarily afford to have me spend a lot of time doing greatly detailed work. I often have to find ways to compromise while still aiming to produce beautiful furniture of sound construction. I look for ways to simplify, to use what tools and materials I can afford and to make limited resources grant handsome returns.

I recently had a challenge of this kind when a client approached me about making a coffee table. Together we settled on a basic table in the Craftsman vein (see the photo above) and a carefully trimmed budget for the job. Two hallmarks of Craftsman furniture are pinned through-mortises and legs coopered or veneered so quartersawn grain shows all around. But I decided to leave them out of my table, substituting the simplicity of loose-tenon joinery and solid-wood construction (see the drawing on p. 44).

LAYING OUT LUMBER

I went looking for about 30 bd. ft. of quartersawn white oak. What I found was a few very rough boards that had turned quite black. After the first pass through my planer, I could see that the wood was not white oak. I was disappointed, but I kept on planing. What emerged was beautiful red oak of a variety I had never seen before. I decided it would suit my purpose well.

With the freshly planed boards arrayed on my outfeed table, I studied the grain and color to decide where the boards would be used to their best advantage. First I selected the boards for the top. These should be picked not only for their beauty but also with an eye toward having even color and straight grain along the edges, so they match well when joined together.

I needed four pieces for the top. I first crosscut them a few inches over length and arranged them as they would be joined. Next I marked a triangle across all four, so I could easily orient them. Then I arranged

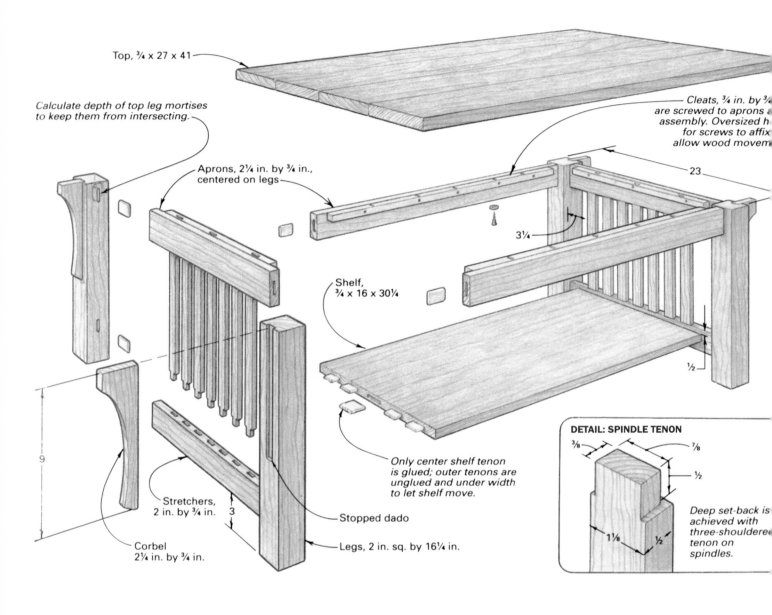

Top, ¾ x 27 x 41

Calculate depth of top leg mortises
to keep them from intersecting.

Aprons, 2¼ in. by ¾ in.,
centered on legs

Cleats, ¾ in. by ¾
are screwed to aprons a
assembly. Oversized h
for screws to affix
allow wood movem

23

3¼

½

Shelf,
¾ x 16 x 30¼

9

Only center shelf tenon
is glued; outer tenons are
unglued and under width
to let shelf move.

Stretchers,
2 in. by ¾ in.   3

Stopped dado

Corbel
2¼ in. by ¾ in.

Legs, 2 in. sq. by 16¼ in.

DETAIL: SPINDLE TENON

⅜   ⅞

½

1⅛   ½

Deep set-back is
achieved with
three-shouldere
tenon on
spindles.

and marked the shelf boards and cut them to rough length.

I don't have a jointer, but with short boards like these, I can get good glue joints by ripping them a few times on the table-saw, taking off about ¹⁄₁₆ in. with each pass and checking them for fit after each cut. For longer stock or waney-edged pieces, I clamp a straightedge to the board and joint it with a flush-trimming router bit.

FLAT TOP

I glued up the top and shelf with pipe clamps, using ¾-in. dowels laid parallel to

the boards as clamping blocks, as shown in the top photo on p. 46. The dowels concentrate the pressure right in the center of the stock and minimize the clamps' tendency to tweak the boards up or down. I keep a stock of dowels of various diameters set aside for this purpose. I find it much easier to grab a pair of the correct size than to hunt down scrap or make up pressure blocks to the thickness of the workpiece each time.

After the glue had set, I beltsanded the slabs. I run my sander diagonally to flatten glued-up panels, feeling for the high spots and concentrating on them to attain a nice, flat surface. I start with a 100-grit belt, first sanding diagonally and then with the grain. Then I change to a 120-grit belt and sand with the grain only. People often complain that a belt sander is hard to control and easy to gouge with, but I have developed a good working relationship with my 3-in. by 21-in. Makita. With practice, you can gain the touch required to flatten a wide surface.

When the beltsanding is finished, I switch to a random-orbit sander and work through the grits, starting with 120 and moving on to 180 and 220. Then I hand-sand with a block and 220-grit paper to remove any slight swirl marks the random orbit may have left. On a relatively forgiving wood like oak, this step is my last, but with something hard and close-grained like cherry, I might finish up with 320-grit paper. Someone once asked me when you know you've sanded enough, and I told him, "You know you never have." There's always more you could do, but it's important to work methodically and take everything to the same level of finish. Instead of beltsanding, you could use handplanes to flatten the top and shelf or rent time on a big thickness sander.

Panels this wide cry out for a panel saw of some kind when it comes to crosscutting, but I don't have one. Instead, I clamp a crosscutting fixture square to the sides and cut one end with a hand-held trim saw, which is a small circular saw. When I had one end straight and square, I made the second cut on the tablesaw about ¼ in. longer than needed. Then I flipped the top around to make a finish cut on the trim-sawn end. I laid out the width so the two outside boards were roughly equal and ripped both sides.

Using this method, I got good tablesaw cuts on all four sides with no tearout. A few strokes with a block plane were all that was needed to clean up the edges.

BUILDING UP LEG STOCK

I glued up the blanks for the legs by sandwiching a piece of ½-in. stock between two ¾-in. pieces. I normally make legs from single sticks, but in this case, I couldn't obtain thick enough stock when I needed it. I took a lot of care with these laminations, matching the layers for color as well as grain orientation. When I was done, the joints were barely perceptible even under close examination. I ripped the 12 pieces for the leg blanks ¼ in. oversized in width and 5 in. oversized in length. The extra width gave me some leeway for slippage during the glue-up and for the final ripping to width. The extra length ensured that any snipe left by the planer in final thicknessing could be cut off.

I arranged the legs carefully, so matching grain would show on each side of the table. Then I held them together, and across the top end grain of the four pieces, I drew a single triangle. This quick marking method makes it easy to establish the orientation of a part at any point in the construction process.

JOINERY

Loose tenoning is the method I use most often for making structural joints because it is strong and straightforward. Also called a splined mortise or floating tenon joint, the loose tenon joint is simply a pair of mating mortises with an independent tenon to span them. With a mortising fixture like mine, as shown in the middle photo on p. 46, the joints are easy to make. Of course, you could also make the mortises by hand, on a router table or with a hollow-chisel mortising setup.

I make loose tenons from the same material as the table, so all seasonal movement will be the same. Just make sure the grain runs the length of the loose tenon. For this table, with 1-in.-wide mortises, I first ripped long strips $^{15}/_{16}$ in. wide and $^7/_{16}$ in. thick. Then I thickness-planed them to exact size, checking them every pass or two in a sample mortise until I got that wonderful feeler-gauge fit. If you have to use strength to pull the spline from the mortise, the fit's too tight; if there's no resistance, it's too loose. Making the tenons $^1/_{16}$ in. undersized in width leaves room for excess glue and also gives you some welcome lateral adjustment in the glue-up. I rounded over the tenon edges on the router table and then cut them to length—$^1/_8$ in. shorter than the combined depth of the two mortises.

DOWELS DELIVER CLAMPING PRESSURE at the center of the board (right), and they keep the glue-up flat. The author keeps dowels of various diameters for gluing different thickness stock.

LOOSE TENONS NEED CLEAN MORTISES. Plunge-routing on a fixture like this shopmade one (above) produces crisp, uniform mortises for the loose tenons.

OFFSET TENONS CREATE A DEEP SET-BACK. For the gallery of spindles on narrow stock, the author offset the tenons, leaving out one shoulder (left).

With all but the shelf and spindle joints cut, I dry-assembled the table. At this point, I measured between the stretchers to find the length of the shelf. This dimension could be calculated, but because even a slight misplacement of a mortise or variation in the thickness of the stretcher could throw everything off, I find it better to measure the length once everything else has been done.

I cut the shelf to size in the same way that I cut the top. It is attached to the stretchers with loose tenons, but only the center tenon is glued. The outer tenons, cut narrow by ⅛ in. and left loose, give the shelf room to move with changes in humidity while supporting it firmly.

The spindles are too small for loose tenons, so I tenoned their ends and cut mat-

ing square mortises in the stretchers and aprons. As I played around with the placement of the spindles, I decided that a ¼-in. set-back from the outside edge of the stretchers and aprons gave it the feeling I wanted. It's surprising what a difference ⅛ in. can make in places like this. If you pull the spindles up to the edge of the rails, you create a flat surface; if you push them in a bit, suddenly the spindles impart a feeling of structure and strength. Given the thickness of the stock I had, this decision meant cutting tenons with no shoulder on the outside face, as shown in the photo at right above. I could have used thicker material for the aprons and stretchers, but none was readily available. So to get the job done and to keep my expenses down, I worked with what I had. I cut the tenons with a dado set on the radial-arm saw.

I chopped mortises for the spindles on the drill press with a ⅜-in. mortising chisel. I wanted the mortises to be ¾ in. by ⅜ in., so I made a ⅜-in. spacer block, which I placed in front of a stop block on the fence. Once the stop block was clamped down at the right spot, I could make a mortise in two quick chops, one with the spacer block and one without. The sides of the mortises required a little cleanup with a chisel, but the ends, which are severed end grain and provide no glue surface, I left rough.

CORBELS

With all the other parts milled and joints cut, I turned to the corbels. These curved supports, borrowed from architecture, are one of the elements that distinguish Craftsman furniture. In this case, they're not structurally significant, but like the deep set-back of the spindles, they lend the piece a sense of weight and solidity. Because I'd left out other decorative details, I wanted to get these right.

I started by making a template. I drew what I felt was a pleasing shape for the corbels on a ½-in. piece of plywood and cut it out with a jigsaw. To fair the curve and rid it of sawmarks, I used a technique I learned from a friend with boatbuilding experience.

I folded sandpaper around a ¹⁄₁₆-in.-thick sliver of wood, as shown in the top photo below. The sliver conforms to the curve, riding over low spots and cutting the high spots. If the initial cut is reasonably true, this quickly produces a perfectly fair curve. Then I used the piece of plywood as a template to shape the corbels. I first jig-sawed the corbels a bit too large and then nailed the template to them with a couple of brads placed in the edge that would be let into the leg. By running the template against a flush-trimming bit in the router table (see the photo below right), I quickly produced identical copies.

The corbels fit into the leg with a stopped dado, which I cut on the tablesaw using a stacked dado blade. I set the fence to position the dado in the center of the leg and clamped a stop block to the fence so that the cut would stop exactly where the corbels end. When the leg hit the stop block, I turned the saw off, waited for the blade to stop and removed the leg. It is quite easy to finish the stopped dado with a chisel.

ASSEMBLY

The corbels were the last parts I made. When they were finished, my favorite moment had arrived—the time for dry-assembly. If all the joints are just right, dry-assembly is a joy to do as everything snaps together and holds tightly without clamps. In this case, I could lift the whole assembly by one leg without anything coming apart. This little act gave me a thrill and impressed my client, who happened to have stopped by my shop at just that moment.

Before final assembly, I block-sanded everything and eased all the edges. Some sanding will always be needed after glue-up, but it is easier to do the bulk of it before-hand when all the pieces lie flat and all their faces are easy to reach.

I did the assembly in stages, first gluing up each end and later linking them together. I started the glue-up by fitting one set of spindles into their stretcher and apron mor-tises. As soon as these joints were pulled tight, I glued the apron and stretcher to the legs. It's important to square this subassembly

by measuring the diagonals with a tape. And I made sure the legs ended up in the same plane by sighting across them. By gluing all this in one operation, I prevented the possi-bility of having a skewed spindle assembly that would not fit neatly into the legs.

When the glue dried, I glued the two side aprons and the shelf between the end frames. I did this on a flat surface, checking the diag-onals again to make sure the table ended up square and making certain all four legs were solidly on the surface. Sometimes a clamp or two must be skewed a bit to achieve this and to ensure the table will not rock later on.

I attached the top with cleats screwed solidly to the apron. To accommodate sea-sonal movement of the top, I drilled over-sized holes up through the cleats and pulled the top tight with pan-head screws fitted with washers.

THE FINISHING TOUCH

For the finish, I applied three coats of Antique Minwax. I rubbed in the final coat with fine steel wool and immediately wiped it off, leaving a beautifully smooth finish that, with occasional reoiling, will only get more beautiful with time.

This table was my first effort in the Craftsman style. I had originally suggested this style to my client because I felt that it would fit the decor and because it stands up so well to heavy use. But while building the table, I came to appreciate the honesty with which design and construction are related in Craftsman work. There is no unnecessary ornamentation—sound structural compo-nents make the design.

SHAPING CORBELS. The author takes down the high spots on the corbel template's jigsawn curve with sandpaper backed by a flexible stick (top).

CORBEL COPIES. A plywood template on the router table (bottom) is used to flush-trim the corbels.

C. MICHAEL VOGT

Bookcase Makes Waves

I finally got fed up trying to fit those big art and architecture books on shallow shelves meant to hold novels. That's why I made the shelves of my freestanding bookcase with serpentine fronts and graduated spacing (see the photo at left). The design is reminiscent of the Craftsman style, especially when made in white oak and fumed with ammonia, as I did.

The case has precise-fitting joints and subtle edge treatments, and though they give the piece a hand-crafted look, the router was the chief tool used. It was indispensable for shaping the shelves, forming tenons and mortising. Templates keep the routing consistent and accurate, and they speeded the whole process.

SERPENTINE-FRONT SHELVES OFFER A GRACE-FUL WAY TO HOLD BOOKS. Although Vogt designed this bookcase so it looks hand-crafted, much of the work is done with a router and templates. The straight components and mortise-and-tenon joinery of the ends, combined with the fumed-oak finish, give the piece a Craftsman flavor.

TUSK-TENONS MAKE THE BOOKCASE EASY TO DISAS-SEMBLE, and because the wedges can be re-tightened at anytime, the joinery makes for a strong connection of the shelves to the ends.

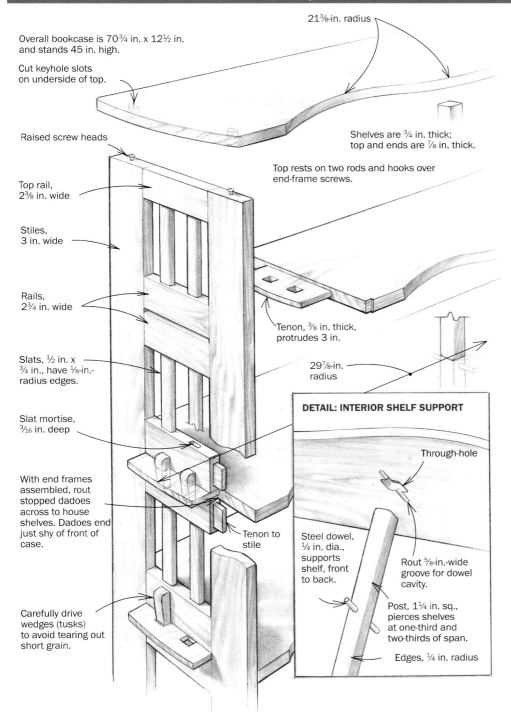

21³⁄₈-in. radius

Overall bookcase is 70³⁄₄ in. x 12½ in. and stands 45 in. high.

Cut keyhole slots on underside of top.

Raised screw heads

Shelves are ¾ in. thick; top and ends are ⅞ in. thick.

Top rail, 2³⁄₈ in. wide

Top rests on two rods and hooks over end-frame screws.

Stiles, 3 in. wide

Rails, 2¾ in. wide

Tenon, ⅜ in. thick, protrudes 3 in.

Slats, ½ in. x ¾ in., have ⅛-in.-radius edges.

29⅞-in. radius

Slat mortise, ³⁄₁₆ in. deep

With end frames assembled, rout stopped dadoes across to house shelves. Dadoes end just shy of front of case.

Tenon to stile

Carefully drive wedges (tusks) to avoid tearing out short grain.

DETAIL: INTERIOR SHELF SUPPORT

Through-hole

Steel dowel, ¼ in. dia., supports shelf, front to back.

Rout ⅝-in.-wide groove for dowel cavity.

Post, 1¼ in. sq., pierces shelves at one-third and two-thirds of span.

Edges, ¼ in. radius

DESIGN AND MATERIALS

To make the bookcase knock down for easy moving, I used tusk-tenon joinery (see the inset opposite). These tenons connect the shelves to the ends. Two posts help hold up the shelves and serve as intermediate book-ends. But because the rods enter each shelf at a single spot, I concealed steel dowels in grooves on the undersides (crossways), to prevent sagging shelves from heavy books.

Choosing stock that's flat and has straight grain is important because cupping would make the joinery difficult to fit and knock

TEMPLATES AND A ROUTER HANDLE SHAPING AND MORTISING. Vogt made a plywood master template so he could form the shelves, complete with tenons, using a straight router bit and a rub collar. The other templates are for shaping the slats, mortises and wedges.

down. The shelf stock is 13 in. wide by 72 in. long. The shelves are ¾ in. thick and the top and ends are ⅞ in. thick.

ROUTING WITH TEMPLATES

Because the router does the lion's share of work in the bookcase, make a good master template for it out of plywood (see the photo at left). Use the template to rout top and shelves to final shape, position the shelves to rout tenons and align the holes and grooves for the posts and dowels. The template is also a convenient surface for drawing full-scale profiles of the case ends, which help to lay out the joinery.

The shelves and top   The top is the same length as the shelves (including their tenons), but it is ½ in. wider. Bandsaw these parts just oversize, and trim them to final size with the template and a flush-trimming router bit. To keep from tearing out grain, climb cut (go with the bit rotation) when advancing the router uphill on the curved front edges. Finish the curves using a spokeshave and scrapers.

You can leave the shelf tenons full thickness, or you can cut ⅛-in.-deep shoulders (as shown in the drawing on p. 47) to reduce the section as it passes through the end frames. With a straight bit and an offset auxiliary base, waste the tenon cheeks, working from the end toward the shoulder, being careful not to tilt the router. Next make the holes for the shelf supports by positioning the template on the underside of the shelf. Mark the square holes, and drill or saw them out, leaving a small amount for the router to trim with a guide bushing and a straight bit. Inserts (see the top photo on p. 51) keep the bit from following the dowel grooves during this operation. When the squares are cut out, remove the spacers, and rout the dowel grooves. Now the shelves and top can be planed, scraped and sanded, and the edges rounded over.

The end frames and slats   The end frames consist of stiles and rails joined by mortises and tenons. Pairs of vertical slats

fill the three frame openings on each side. After you've cut all the end-frame pieces to size, clamp the frames together, and rout and chisel stopped dadoes on the inside for the shelves. The rails contact the shelves' through-tenons (top and bottom) on the outside, and the dadoes receive the shelves on the inside.

Actually, the dadoes are rabbets at the inner edges of the rails. The depth and width of the dadoes must be precise so that the shelves will fit tightly and the tusk tenons will be under tension from their wedges. To waste the rail tenons that enter the end stiles, measure back from the front stile edges to determine where the tenons pass through. Then saw away the waste. Leave enough room for the tenons to expand side to side.

Instead of cutting shouldered tenons for the slats, I housed them in mortises routed with a template. I used another template to form the slats. I rounded over the slat edges to match the radius of the mortises. After the slats have been cut to length, scraped and sanded, I clamp the frames with slats, and test-fit the shelves.

The posts and dowels   Make the posts slightly smaller than their holes; the posts' edges are rounded to match the radii of the corners of the holes. Hold the posts next to an end frame, and mark lines at the bottom edges of the shelves. Measure the exact depth the dowel grooves will be and drill all the holes through the posts. It's best to use a drill press and stop blocks for this.

TUSK-TENONS AND WEDGES

While the case is clamped tightly, shelves in place, scribe from the outside where the tenons pass through the frames. Remove the shelves, and use the tenon template to mark the mortises. Drill out the bulk of the mortises, and use an angled block and chisel to pare the sloping shoulders. Undercut the innermost edges. Lightly chamfer around the edges of the mortises, so the wedges won't catch any grain going in and out (see the drawing on p. 49). Use the wedge template to mark the wedges. Saw them out, clean up the sawmarks, test for fit, and shape the edges and ends.

For the end-frame assembly, use a slow-setting glue. Then when installing the shelves, carefully drive the wedges so that you don't split out the shelf ends.

The top fits onto the end frames with a sheet-metal screw and a T-slot. I made two keyhole slots on each end to align with four screws centered in the top of the stiles (see the drawing detail). Let the top move separately from the end frames because the rails have grain running crossways.

FUMING AND FINISHING

This bookcase was fumed with ammonia to darken the oak, but the piece takes on an entirely different look when you use other finishes. For example, I painted one white for a light appearance, and I varnished another for a natural look.

If you fume with ammonia, it's healthier to do it outdoors. If, instead, you make a fuming chamber for the shop, as I did (see the photo at right), be sure to exhaust the fumes outside to minimize your exposure to the noxious gas. I sized my chamber to the bookcase and put trays for the ammonia in the bottom. Polyethylene wraps the framework top, back and sides. And duct tape laps all the seams. The chamber is on casters, so I can roll it out of the way. The front door is plastic-covered and screwed over the opening. For a seal, I used closed-cell weather stripping on the door back. I bought concentrated (28%) ammonia from a blueprint supply company.

During fuming, the wood closest to the ammonia darkened more than the rest, so I placed a small fan (available at heating supply stores) inside to circulate the fumes more evenly. I keep the tray bottoms barely covered with ammonia and judge the wood's color over a day or two. Ideally, all the ammonia in the trays will evaporate, but to make things safer, turn on the exhaust fan, and crack the door a bit. After I retrieved my bookcase (without shedding a tear), I applied five coats of Waterlox oil/varnish to the piece.

STEEL DOWELS IN ROUTED SLOTS REINFORCE THE SHELVES. With the template flipped, the author will rout through-mortises for posts and rout grooves for dowels. The lauan overlay strips allow for the thickness of the guide bushing. The inserts are removable.

FUMING WITH AMMONIA ADDS DRAMATIC COLOR and highlights the grain of oak but requires a chamber. A polyethylene-covered frame holds trays that will be partially filled with concentrated ammonia and the door will be sealed.

REX ALEXANDER

Stickley
Done Lightly

Craftsman-style furniture is traditionally made of fumed, quartersawn white oak. Gustav Stickley was one of the champions of the Craftsman movement, and his name is synonymous with a distinctive style of blocky, muscular furniture. In Stickley's 1909 book *Craftsman Homes,* he talks about native woods and how to use them. "Oak is a robust, manly sort of wood and is most at home in large rooms which are meant for constant use, such as the living room, reception hall, library or dining room."

The oak version of the table shown here was first featured on the cover of *Fine Woodworking #122.* That photo illustrated my article about building an Arts-and-Crafts side chair. After the article was published, I received many calls—not about the chair, but regarding the table.

One client wanted a lighter, more feminine pick of wood: figured maple. She chose a design I had already used for an oak table. Its inspiration came from Stickley's No. 657 library table and Frank Lloyd Wright's rectilinear furniture. With a top measuring 48 in. by 110 in., it's meant for entertaining large groups. Even with bulky legs to support its mass, the use of curly

Square spindles, round tenons

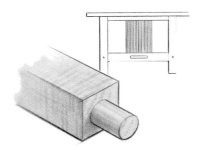

Making the spindles round in a PVC pipe jig on the radial-arm saw is faster than using traditional methods for machining square tenons.

CUTTING ROUND TENONS ON SQUARE STOCK. Slip two pieces of PVC pipe over a spindle. Carefully rotate the spindle against the radial-arm saw's fence and a stop block while moving the cutter-head, fitted with a dado blade, to remove the waste. ■

maple (finished in a light tone) gives the table a more feminine, lighter presence.

Birds-eye maple was my customer's wood of choice. But I knew it would be nearly impossible to find birds-eye in the large dimensions required 8/4 in. thick and 10 ft. long. We settled on curly maple. Birds-eye was selected as a secondary wood, and its use was limited to the spindles.

BUYING LUMBER BY THE LOG ALLOWS BOOK-MATCHING

Finding 200 bd. ft. of curly maple in the lengths I needed also proved to be difficult, so I sought out a timber broker and sawyer. I decided to buy whole logs and have them resawn, which would take extra work and time. But it was worth the trouble because I was able to tell the sawyer just how I wanted the logs cut. Using wood from the same tree guaranteed that I would be able to match the figure and color.

My customer told me that she didn't want her table to appear "too bossy," that is, she didn't want it too wild with figure. So I had the logs flitchsawn (sawed completely through in successive layers). This method yields a combination of flat or tangential grain and quartersawn or radial grain. I ended up with boards that had a lot of curl in the quartersawn areas and calmer grain in the flatsawn areas. The areas of greatest curl were on the outside edges of the log.

I like to use air-dried wood because it machines cleaner, with less tearout. But air drying, I was told, wasn't an option with the curly maple. Curl is actually an abnormality to maple, and it causes stress in the wood. Kiln drying, I was told, would help stabilize the maple. Well, I hate to imagine what that stack of lumber would have looked like if I had air dried it. Curly maple was an apt description of the lumber's condition after kiln drying (for more on flattening lumber, see pp. 56-57).

VARIATIONS ON A STICKLEY THEME

The grain—rays or flecks—found in premium quartersawn oak adds visual interest to Stickley's rather simple furniture. I used curly maple to achieve a similar effect by matching up the most-figured planks and gluing them up for the massive top.

Stickley was a stickler for uniform figure on his work. Because legs made of solid stock only show quartersawn figure on two sides, he solved the problem by making legs from four mitered quartersawn sections. Some people solve the problem by simply gluing quartersawn veneer on two faces. Because this table has an altogether different look and feel from standard Stickley, I laminated two pieces of 8/4 book-matched stock for the legs and left it at that.

The spindles are best machined after you have dry-fit their matching components, which I use to mark off the location of the tenons. I machine round tenons on the ends of the spindles using a radial-arm saw, a dado blade and two short sections of PVC pipe that allow me to rotate the stock evenly.

Using the assembled rails as a marking guide, I lay out the tenons on a piece of scrap spindle stock to set up my radial-arm saw. I fit the radial-arm saw with a dado blade and position a stop block to establish the tenon's length. Before cutting, I slip a piece of plastic pipe over each end of a spindle, keeping the ends exposed. Be sure there is no slop in the fit. I place the stock against the stop block and back fence and make a cut (see the photos on p. 54). Then I rotate the spindle about 90° and make successive cuts to all four sides to remove most of the waste. I round over the tenons by carefully spinning the spindle/pipe fixture against the stop block and fence while moving the dado head back and forth.

Hidden beneath the tabletop is a subtop, a piece of ¾-in. plywood with solid maple edges (cross ties) on two sides. A subtop has several purposes: It houses the mortises for the spindles attached to the stretcher, keeps the long side rails from flexing and helps keep the top flat. The subtop is screwed and glued to the rabbet in the long upper rails (see the photos above). Two vertical supports, which are mortised into the stretcher, are screwed to the cross ties of the subtop.

The subtop, as well as rails, are drilled out for screws to fasten the top. The large top will move considerably with seasonal changes in humidity, so I make the screw holes wide enough to allow the screws to move with the wood. I drill 1-in.-dia. holes 1⅝ in. deep from the top of the aprons with a Forstner bit. From the bottom of the apron, I drill toward the 1-in. holes using a #8 countersink bit.

■ Subtop keeps the base from racking

The subtop, a piece of ¾-in. plywood with solid edges glued to two sides, fits into a rabbet cut into the long upper rails of the table's base. Four large holes in the subtop house screws that hold the tabletop in place. The holes are larger at the top than at the bottom to allow the screws to move as the tabletop adjusts to seasonal changes in humidity.

SCREW AND GLUE SUBTOP TO RAILS. The author squares up a slight misalignment in the base using a pipe clamp, then glues and screws the subtop in place.

A RECIPE FOR FINISHING

Before applying the finish, I use a Stanley No. 80 scraper; then I sand beginning with 220-grit, going through 600-grit. All edges are relieved slightly using a block plane or file and sandpaper.

I use a combination of oils, polyurethane and beeswax. First I heat boiled linseed oil in a pan on an electric hot plate outside my shop. Just before it begins to smoke (usually at about 120°F), I remove it from the burner and liberally apply it to the table and base with a rag using rubber gloves to protect my hands. After about 20 minutes, I wipe it off and let it dry for 24 hours. I repeat the process two more times for a total of three coats. After the last coat of linseed oil has dried for three days, I apply three coats of an equal mixture of tung oil and polyurethane, letting each dry for 24 hours.

My top finish coat consists of equal parts beeswax, tung oil and boiled linseed oil. I melt the beeswax in a double boiler, remove it from the heat and add the other ingredients. When the mixture cools, it develops a creamy texture. I apply that with my hand and wipe it off with a rag. After a day, I'll apply one more coat and buff it with a clean cloth.

No jointer? No problem

I made the mistake of purchasing a used light-duty jointer many years ago. For several months the machine tugged on my patience because it would not heed my commands to mill lumber flat. Then I made peace with it. I distanced myself from this dog of a tool, which now lies in its own corner of the shop, its bite and growl silenced, the unplugged power cord curled peacefully about its legs.

Long planks, such as the 10-ft. pieces used to make up the Stickley tabletop, present a difficult milling challenge when they are warped and twisted. Jointing them flat can waste much material. I relied on my carpentry background and tools to solve the problem.

2. In cabinet work, I often have to scribe a flat cabinet to fit a warped wall. I flipped the concept on its head and found a way to scribe a crooked board using a flat surface for reference. Then I use the scribe marks to guide a powered hand planer and flatten one face.

Use a tablesaw and its long outfeed table to serve as a guide for scribing warped stock. It's important that you take the time to level the outfeed table to the exact height of the tablesaw. Also, make sure the table's surface doesn't suffer from dips or other imperfections.

When a plank is badly warped, balance it on the outfeed table and tablesaw using weights or blocks of wood to prevent one corner from sitting too high. So when you scribe, you end up splitting the difference between high and low spots.

1. Before you begin to scribe, you need a fairly flat surface on the edge of a board to write on. If the edge is rough and ragged, snap a line and cut off the waste with a circular saw. The opposite edge can then be ripped straight on the tablesaw. Trim the ends as well.

3. After scribing, flip the plank over, and remove waste with a power planer, paying close attention to the scribed line. Finish up using a No. 7 jointer plane. To check your progress, flip the plank over onto the outfeed table and see if it rocks.

You don't have to completely flatten every square inch of the plank before resorting to a thickness planer to true the other side. As long as the plank won't rock as it goes through a planer, the other face can be trued. You do have to remove any bow because a thickness planer can temporarily compress the bow out of a board as it passes through. Once the second face is true, flip it over, and send the first face through the machine to clean it up.

4. Squaring an edge comes next. Because I don't own a working jointer, I have an alternative method for jointing. I chuck the board in a vise and use a power hand planer fitted with a homemade carriage that keeps the tool square to the edge. Take light passes and sight along the edge to check your progress.

5. A power planer can only get you so far. I get a good glue edge by jointing stock on a router table. My router is attached under the side extension of my tablesaw, which allows me to use the table-saw's fence for routing, too. For jointing, I made an adjustable, auxiliary fence that fits over my rip fence.

I use pieces of ¾-in.-thick melamine for my auxiliary fence and attach it to the saw fence using L-brackets and carriage bolts. Alternatively, you can use an adjustable router-table fence that allows you to offset one-half of the fence relative to the other. To joint a board, adjust both fences in the same plane, and then adjust the rip fence to take off only ¹⁄₃₂ in. Joint a few inches of a board, turn off the router and reposition the outfeed half of the auxiliary fence flush against the jointed section.

I've had good results jointing edges using a ½-in. solid-carbide up-cut spiral bit or a ¾-in. carbide-tipped straight bit. After jointing one edge, rip the other side using the tablesaw, and joint that edge on the router. Correct any slight imperfections using a No. 7 jointer plane. Then slightly hollow out the center of each glue edge with a scraper to avoid a starved joint. I don't use biscuits or splines to align boards. I do, however, glue up only two or three planks at a time so that I don't go crazy trying to keep everything flat.

6. After letting a panel dry overnight, I use a No. 80 cabinet scraper to remove gluelines and any tearout left by the power tools. On a tabletop this big, it's easier to just hop aboard, and go to work on your hands and knees.

MORTISE-AND-TENON CONSTRUCTION IS REINFORCED WITH PINS AND SCREWS.

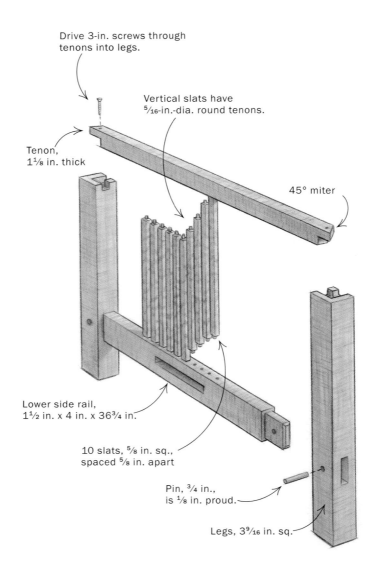

Drive 3-in. screws through tenons into legs.

Vertical slats have $^5/_{16}$-in.-dia. round tenons.

Tenon, $1^1/_8$ in. thick

45° miter

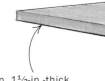

Top, $1^1/_2$-in.-thick curly maple

Lower side rail, $1^1/_2$ in. x 4 in. x $36^3/_4$ in.

10 slats, $^5/_8$ in. sq., spaced $^5/_8$ in. apart

Pin, $^3/_4$ in., is $^1/_8$ in. proud.

Legs, $3^9/_{16}$ in. sq.

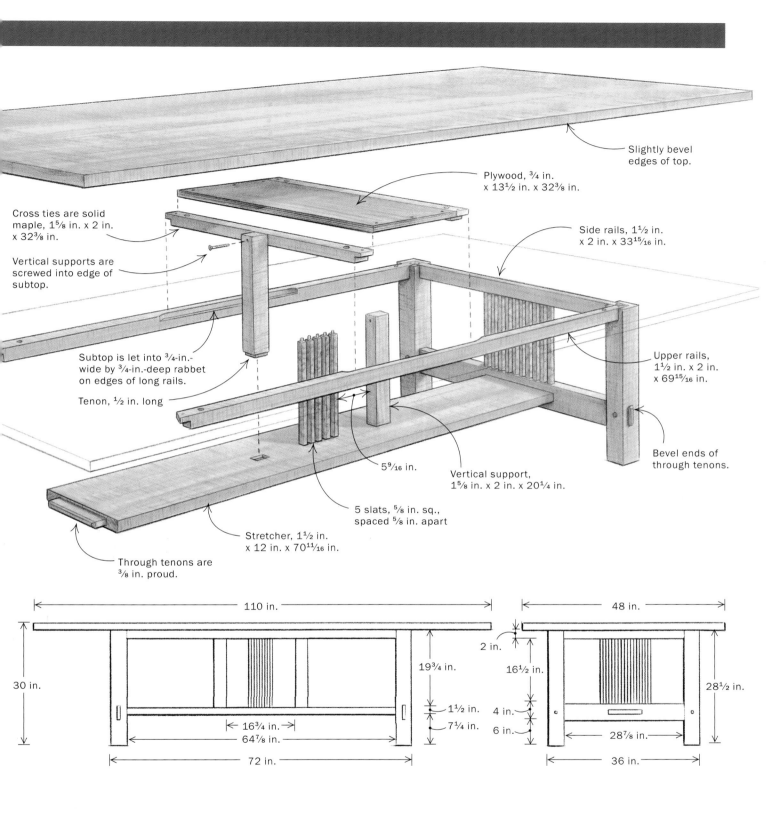

Slightly bevel edges of top.

Plywood, ¾ in. x 13½ in. x 32⅜ in.

Cross ties are solid maple, 1⅝ in. x 2 in. x 32⅜ in.

Vertical supports are screwed into edge of subtop.

Side rails, 1½ in. x 2 in. x 33¹⁵⁄₁₆ in.

Subtop is let into ¾-in.-wide by ¾-in.-deep rabbet on edges of long rails.

Tenon, ½ in. long

Upper rails, 1½ in. x 2 in. x 69¹⁵⁄₁₆ in.

Bevel ends of through tenons.

5⁹⁄₁₆ in.

Vertical support, 1⅝ in. x 2 in. x 20¼ in.

5 slats, ⅝ in. sq., spaced ⅝ in. apart

Stretcher, 1½ in. x 12 in. x 70¹¹⁄₁₆ in.

Through tenons are ⅜ in. proud.

110 in.

48 in.

2 in.

30 in.

19¾ in.

16½ in.

1½ in.

7¼ in.

4 in.

6 in.

28½ in.

16¾ in.

64⅞ in.

72 in.

28⅞ in.

36 in.

ERIC KEIL

Hefty Sofa Table with a Delicate Touch

Of the 23 pieces of furniture I made for a house in the Pennsylvania Poconos, this sofa table was the most gratifying to build and the best designed. Large members make up the tabletop and legs, and a 5/4 cabinet rests below. It's a hefty design built in a light, natural cherry, with unique exposed joinery that complements other furniture I installed in the home. The table's effect is at once traditional and contemporary, as are the processes used to build it.

The sofa table is my favorite piece in the house, but I did have a few concerns with the initial design. I spoke with Robert McLaughlin, the architect who designed the

BREADBOARDS WITH A TWIST. The unique breadboard design of the tabletop calls for the long side boards to sandwich the short end boards.

table, and it was apparent that he had a lot of woodworking savvy. He anticipated many of my concerns and accepted some compromises to improve the joinery and chances that the table age gracefully.

DESIGN COMPROMISES

As I looked at the preliminary drawings, there were three unconventional design elements that seemed troublesome. The configuration of the boards that made up the top was specific and unusual: two 2-in. by 5-in. pieces surrounded by a butt-jointed frame. Instead of a traditional breadboard design, the long outermost side boards sandwiched the end boards. This kind of joinery with solid lumber would have caused the joints between the end boards and the center of the table to fail over time. The architect had no problem with my solution to replace the center pieces with a stable substrate and veneer.

Another concern was that the design called for the legs to come through the top in a full through-tenon. Even if I consistently and accurately cut the mortises and through-tenons on the legs, I couldn't comfortably glue and clamp the top to the assembled cabinet and legs below. And housing the solid legs in a veneered substrate wouldn't allow for seasonal wood movement. We decided to make the tenons false. The legs would butt the bottom of the tabletop, and corresponding end-grain

**HOUSE AND FURNITURE SHARE COMMON ELE-
MENTS.** Working with large timbers raised concerns
for the author. What appears to be a solid-board top
is actually a clever sandwich of MDF and veneer.
Through-mortised legs are another clever deception.
The breadboard ends (facing page) also have an
unusual design.

▪ Tabletop has heart of MDF

VENEER SANDWICHES MDF. Three layers of MDF and two layers of veneer are all coated in glue and set into the vacuum bag at the same time. Glued up slightly oversized, the entire center panel of the tabletop is later trimmed to size on the tablesaw.

SHORT ENDS FIRST. Fitted with a spline and biscuits, the short ends of the table are clamped to the top. With the end boards glued into place, a spline is cut slightly short of the top's length.

TIGHT SPLINES ARE EXPOSED. Small lengths of spline are tapped into place to ensure that the conspicuous table ends fit tightly. ▪

inserts could be carefully fit to shallow mortises on the top of the table.

The carcase of the cabinet itself was to be made of 5/4 solid cherry boards. The design called for the cabinet to be joined at the corners with an oversized finger or box joint. The fingers were 4 in. wide, corresponding with the seams between each 4-in.-wide board and its neighbor. The problem with this design was that the only long-grain-to-long-grain glue bond occurs every 4 in., which simply isn't sufficient.

When working with heavy timbers and on such a grand scale, it's imperative that the stock be stabilized and milled to exact size.

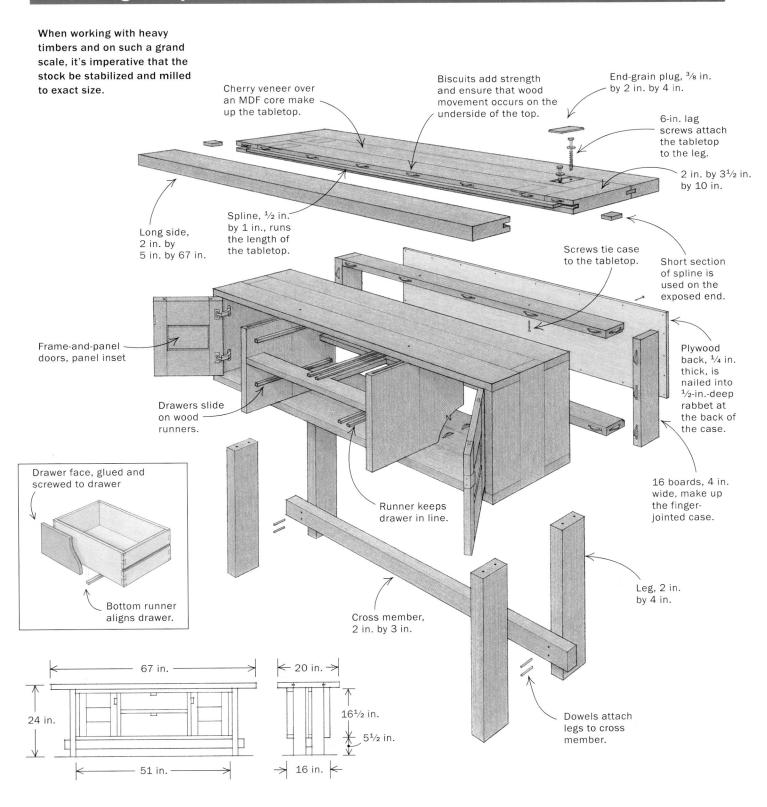

Cherry veneer over an MDF core make up the tabletop.

Biscuits add strength and ensure that wood movement occurs on the underside of the top.

End-grain plug, ³/₈ in. by 2 in. by 4 in.

6-in. lag screws attach the tabletop to the leg.

2 in. by 3¹/₂ in. by 10 in.

Long side, 2 in. by 5 in. by 67 in.

Spline, ¹/₂ in. by 1 in., runs the length of the tabletop.

Screws tie case to the tabletop.

Short section of spline is used on the exposed end.

Frame-and-panel doors, panel inset

Plywood back, ¹/₄ in. thick, is nailed into ¹/₂-in.-deep rabbet at the back of the case.

Drawers slide on wood runners.

Runner keeps drawer in line.

16 boards, 4 in. wide, make up the finger-jointed case.

Drawer face, glued and screwed to drawer

Bottom runner aligns drawer.

Cross member, 2 in. by 3 in.

Leg, 2 in. by 4 in.

Dowels attach legs to cross member.

67 in.

20 in.

24 in.

16¹/₂ in.

5¹/₂ in.

51 in.

16 in.

■ Finger-jointed carcase

A RACE AGAINST CURING GLUE. The cabinet must be glued up in one swift process. Four-board boxes are biscuited, coated in white glue, then set onto similar assemblies.

PLUNGE-CUT THE GROOVE. To cut a groove, the biscuit machine slides like a router along the edge of the divider.

LIKE A HAND IN A GLOVE. Biscuits are glued into the cabinet frame, then the grooved divider slides easily into place. ■

I added two biscuits to each finger (dowels or splines could have been used instead), which solved the problem of insufficient bonding surface but created another dilemma that I will address later.

AN UNCONVENTIONAL TABLETOP

The tabletop's 2-in.-thick center was made by laminating three pieces of medium-density fiberboard (MDF)—two pieces ¾ in. thick and one piece ⅜ in. thick—then skinning both sides with 1/16-in.-thick cherry veneer. I glued up the veneer in two pieces so that it appears to be two 5-in.-wide boards. The veneer was cut about ¾ in. oversized on the tablesaw and then seamed. Making the substrate, cauls and veneer the same approximate size allowed for easy alignment and control of the pieces as they went into the vacuum bag. It was also quicker and less obnoxious to trim the ¾-in. oversized panels on a tablesaw than it would have been to trim glue squeeze-out and oversized veneer with a router and trimmer bit.

Placing the vacuum bag on an absolutely flat surface and laminating multiple layers of the substrate material produced a flat panel with no warp, cup or twist. After several hours in the vacuum bag, the veneered panel needed only a quick cleanup before it was cut to size. Trying to get clean edges of MDF on a jointer is fruitless, and it dulls knives instantly. So I measured out from the centerline (seam) of the top veneers to establish parallel lines, then tacked a straightedge to the unexposed bottom surface. I ripped the panel several times on the tablesaw until I was sure the edges were straight, square and parallel, but I left them about ¼ in. oversized for now.

I used the tablesaw to crosscut the panel to length, again taking several test passes to check the quality of cut. If the veneer was going to chip, it would be at the end of a crosscut. I ripped the panel to its final width last, which ensured crisp corners. When ripping, raising the blade higher than normal produces a cleaner top cut (and

ROBERT McLAUGHLIN

A WORD FROM THE ARCHITECT

I've always tried to create houses and furniture that express the nature of both the materials and the construction process. Whether it's exposing bolts in steelwork or leaving the joinery uncovered in wood, the effect is always powerful.

The monumental scale of some of the rooms in the house led principal architect Peter Bohlin and me to these furniture designs. We needed sizable legs and cross members so that the furniture wouldn't seem lost against the 9-in. square columns that frame the house. We also designed overlapping and penetrating connections to match the Arts-and-Crafts or Japanese-like joinery seen throughout the home. It was clear early on that Eric Keil understood the styles that we were trying to create.

One aspect of this project that was amazingly successful was the collaboration between an owner, a craftsman and designers. Often, when too many people become involved in a project, the outcome becomes diluted. But that never happened. All parties were involved at each phase of the work, including full-sized mock-ups to see how the pieces would fit in the room. The work between Eric and me was almost always hands-on. I'd visit his shop at least every other week, and sometimes more.

Toward the end of the project, our sketches to Eric consisted only of the major dimensions and no notes. Eric knew what we wanted, and we trusted his judgment, so we didn't have to waste time mapping out every detail. This process led to the successful execution of all of the furniture, including this sofa table.

A MEETING OF MINDS. Furniture maker Eric Keil (right) and architect Robert McLaughlin discuss concerns about the sofa table's design.

coarser bottom cut) because of the related angle at which the saw cuts through the material. When cutting with a raised blade, be sure the blade guard is in place.

I milled the solid frame pieces ½ in. thicker than the center panel. This, along with careful glue-up, made it easier to hand-plane the massive frame flush to the veneer. Frame members were cut to length and then grooved on the tablesaw. Although spline joinery by itself might have been sufficient, I added biscuits above the spline so that any discrepancies in flushness would show on the unexposed bottom of the tabletop rather than on top.

Because of the relative sloppiness of biscuit joinery, excess glue got trapped in the joint when the tabletop was glued up. This, coupled with the swelling of the biscuits, meant that I had to allow the swelling to go down before working the tabletop. Sanding or scraping the surface before the swelling had subsided would have left biscuit-shaped depressions in the finish.

After I milled splines to fit the grooves, I beveled the corners slightly to ease assembly. Splines can also be milled a little shy in width to allow excess glue to escape—and to ensure that the visible top joints pull tight. I cut the long splines 2 in. short in length so that the exposed spline could be hand-fitted. During clamping, I used a straightedge to make sure the slightly proud faces of the solid frame were parallel to the center panel.

Where the splines are exposed on the end of the table, a 1-in. length of spline was tightly fitted and set into place. I did this before the glue from the tabletop assembly had a chance to harden, eliminating the need to chisel dried glue out of the mortise. I tapped the 1-in. spline home, trimmed it flush and left the assembly to set overnight.

FAUX FINGER JOINTS

The 16-in.-deep cabinet under the sofa table was the most labor intensive part of the project. When I make a finger-jointed box, I typically cut the sides to size, machine the joinery and assemble it all at once. But this cabinet wouldn't go together that way. I decided to make it by stacking four 4-in.-deep butt-jointed boxes (see the photos on p. 64). Alternately butted and stacked, the boxes create a strong cabinet.

Rather than gluing up each of the four boxes separately and then stacking them in a subsequent operation, I had to glue together the 16 individual pieces at the same time. The process is nerve-racking and fast paced, but it was much easier to manipulate 16 loose pieces than to try to force four rigid boxes to come together as one. Slow-setting white glue, calm preparation and special clamping blocks helped everything go smoothly. I also cut the biscuit slots so that the exposed end grain would be a hair proud.

After flushing up these end-grain surfaces with a jack plane, I was ready to make the interior dividers. By using a biscuit machine as a groove cutter, I was able to slide the interior dividers into place after the exterior box had been assembled. After that, the cabinet needed only a quick scraping and some final sanding.

END-GRAIN INSERTS IN THE TABLETOP

The legs were doweled to the cross member that supports the cabinet, then set into place under the tabletop. Waiting to cut mortises until the legs were attached to the cabinet ensured that the end-grain inserts would align with the legs below. A router with a template guide and a small-diameter straight-cutting bit made it easy to cut the mortises (see the top photo on the facing page). The small-diameter bit reduced the radius of the mortise corners, so I only had to chop them square with a chisel.

In a previous project with the same detail, I made the end-grain inserts too thin. During clamping, glue worked its way to the top surface. The glue-saturated pieces had to be removed and redone—a lesson not soon forgotten. This time, I left the ⅜-in.-thick end-grain inserts a hair thicker than the depth of the mortises so that I could plane them flush later.

With a lower assembly of such weight, I worried that small screws would pull away from the MDF if the table was lifted by the top. To be safe, I used lag screws. The mortises for the end-grain inserts were drilled to accept 6-in. lag screws and washers. After attaching the tabletop to the lower assembly, the holes were filled to the bottom of the mortises with auto-body filler (see the middle photo at right). This eliminated any swelling caused by pockets of excess glue. It also prohibited any metal-to-glue contact that might discolor the end-grain inserts. I didn't use common wood fillers because they tend to shrink, which would have left depressions in the tabletop.

I carefully fit the inserts and fine-tuned them with a rigid sanding block. Yellow glue might eventually fail, allowing the inserts to pull away from their housings, so I coated the end-grain inserts with polyurethane glue and clamped them tightly into place (see the bottom photo at right).

A FINAL TOUCH

I made two frame-and-panel doors and dovetailed maple drawers with cherry bottoms. They were then fitted and sanded. Doors were hung on concealed hinges, and drawers were fitted to maple slides.

I finished the entire table with a coat of vinyl sealer and two light coats of catalyzed lacquer sprayed on with low-pressure system. I cut the lacquer and sealer with retarder thinner, which allows more time for a finish to level out. The retarder thinner also prevents the more porous veins in the wood from filling up, leaving a more natural appearance, akin to that of an oil finish.

Four years after I made the piece, the sofa table looks as pristine as it did the day it was delivered. The techniques utilized seem to have been time worthy. When I reflect on this project, I still get gratification from how tightly crafted this table is. Another thing that makes this table so intriguing is the weight of the large cherry timbers and Robert McLaughlin's design. In the large room where it lives, the table appears to grow gracefully from the floor.

■ Inserts mimic through-tenons

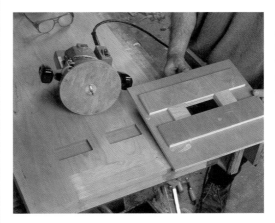

MORTISES THAT MATCH. A small-diameter straight-cutting bit and a simple template make easy work of cutting the mortises in the tabletop.

BOLTS AND BONDO. The tabletop is secured to the legs with 6-in. lag screws, then covered with auto-body filler. More common wood fillers might shrink, leaving depressions in the tabletop.

FAUX LEG ENDS. End-grain inserts are coated with polyurethane glue and then tapped into place. ■

GARY ROGOWSKI

Building an Arts-and-Crafts Sideboard (Part I)

When I was asked to build a sideboard that had a Greene and Greene feel to it, I decided to use an original piece as a springboard for my own interpretation. But I wanted to do more than just copy something designed in the early 1900s by these famous brothers.

I tried to soak up as much visual information on the style as I could. I pored over designs of the Greene brothers and their contemporaries. Then I closed all the books and sat down at the drawing board. What I came up with is more contemporary and less ornate than the Greenes' work (see the photo below). This sideboard, made of Honduras mahogany, had to work as a backdrop for my inlay work as well as have the overall grace of a Greene and Greene piece. I didn't want it to dominate a room.

It's mind-boggling how many pieces, joints and cuts are in this sideboard. The key to successful completion of this project

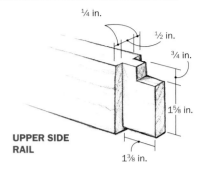

Construction of this sideboard begins with the two end assemblies. Lower side rail tenons are the same as the upper side rail tenons except that they're not haunched.

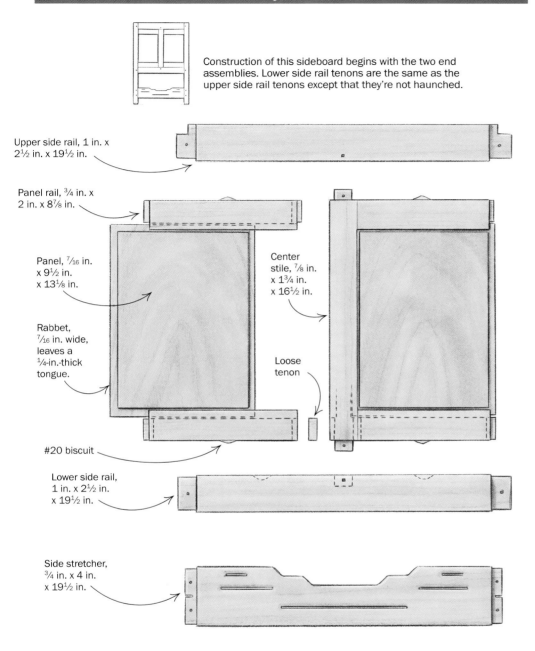

Upper side rail, 1 in. x 2½ in. x 19½ in.

Panel rail, ¾ in. x 2 in. x 8⅞ in.

Panel, ⁷⁄₁₆ in. x 9½ in. x 13⅛ in.

Center stile, ⅞ in. x 1¾ in. x 16½ in.

Rabbet, ⁷⁄₁₆ in. wide, leaves a ¼-in.-thick tongue.

Loose tenon

#20 biscuit

Lower side rail, 1 in. x 2½ in. x 19½ in.

Side stretcher, ¾ in. x 4 in. x 19½ in.

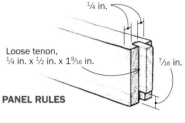

¼ in.
½ in.
¾ in.
1⅝ in.
1⅜ in.

UPPER SIDE RAIL

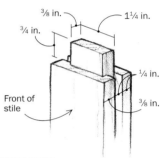

¼ in.

Loose tenon, ¼ in. x ½ in. x 1⁹⁄₁₆ in.

⁷⁄₁₆ in.

PANEL RULES

⅜ in.
1¼ in.
¾ in.
¼ in.
⅜ in.

Front of stile

CENTER STILE

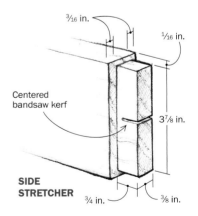

³⁄₁₆ in.
¹⁄₁₆ in.

Centered bandsaw kerf

3⅞ in.

SIDE STRETCHER

¾ in.
⅜ in.

is breaking it down into manageable sections and then figuring out how to splice them together.

That's how I planned construction of this sideboard, beginning here through p. 95. After I worked out an overall design, I concentrated on the structure of the carcase, which is the subject here (pp. 68-77). The next consideration was the interior of the piece—how the drawers would be supported and how the doors would be hung. That's covered on pp. 78-85. Finally, there are the details—knobs, pulls, carved inlay and other decoration that make a piece distinctive. You'll find all of that discussed on pp. 86-95.

The more planning, drawings and design work you do up front, the fewer headaches

ROUTER JIG SPEEDS AND SIMPLIFIES JOINERY. The author used a Multi-Router to rout all the mortises and tenons on this sideboard. Grooves, dadoes and dovetail slots were done on a router table or with a handheld router. Dovetails were cut by hand. ■

you'll have later. I find it more than worthwhile to do full-scale joinery drawings; they help me avoid unpleasant surprises.

MILLWORK LAYS THE FOUNDATION

A poorly laid foundation for a house causes problems from framing to finishing. Similarly, if you build a piece of furniture with stock that's not straight and square, you're bound to run into trouble.

First I rough-mill the stock and let it acclimate to my shop. I cut boards to within ½ in. of finished length and joint one face and an edge. I leave stock ⅛ in. over in

width and thickness. Then I sticker all the boards for a few days. If any boards cup, bow, twist or check, they're replaced. I take the boards down to their finished dimensions when I need to cut the joinery.

The millwork for the ⁷⁄₁₆-in.-thick side panels in each end of the sideboard took some extra thought. I could have planed down 4/4 boards, but half of each board would have ended up in my dust collector. Instead, I resawed 5/4 stock. Because my bandsaw can resaw boards only up to 8 in. wide, I ripped the 10-in.-wide material in half, resawed these pieces and then glued mating pieces back together. This gave me two book-matched panels about ½ in. thick for each side with perfectly matching grain.

BEGIN THE CARCASE WITH THE ENDS

Each end assembly consists of a dozen pieces. I routed all the mortises and tenons, using a Multi-Router (see the photo at left), although the joinery certainly could be cut in a number of other ways. First I cut and fit the center stile tenons to the mortises in the upper and lower side rails. Then, with a ¼-in. bit in my router table, I routed the grooves for the loose tenons that connect the panel rails to the center stile. Using the same router-table setup, I roughed out the panel grooves in the center stile and panel rails. I did the final routing of these grooves when the sideboard ends were dry-assembled. The stopped grooves for the loose tenons in the legs had to be marked and cut separately on the router table.

With the work on the center stiles done, I glued them between upper and lower side rails. I fitted each panel rail between leg and stile and then routed the grooves for the loose tenons that connect the panel rails to the legs. After giving all the rails a quick sanding, I glued the panel rails to the stile with loose tenons and to the upper and lower side rails with one #20 biscuit. If any of the panel-rail shoulders don't line up perfectly with the side-rail shoulders, you can trim them later with a rabbet plane.

Grooving for the side panels The grooves for the panels have to line up all the way around the frame. Rather than routing each piece separately and hoping that the panel grooves lined up at the corners, I dry-assembled the frame to rout grooves in it with a ¼-in. slot cutter. To give the router a level platform, I put spacers on the side rails and center stile (see the top photo on the right). I also screwed a wooden block to the router subbase so I couldn't tip the router in the cut.

I rabbeted the panels on the router table and then handplaned the backs until they fit perfectly. I sanded and finished the panels with three coats of wiping varnish. I also finished the inside edges of the legs, panel rails and center stiles—all places that would be difficult to finish after the end assemblies were glued up.

Before leaping into a glue-up, I put a ½-in.-long 14° bevel on the foot of each leg and drilled holes for the dowel pins and the ebony plugs used to pin the mortise-and-tenon joints (see the drawing on p. 74). I also routed the dovetail slot at the top of the leg for the top front rail and laid out the dovetail in the rail from the slot.

Template-routing the stretchers The last piece for each side assembly was a stretcher. With so many curves and routed grooves in them, templates seemed the best way to shape the stretchers. I made the templates out of ¼-in. hardboard, roughing them out on the bandsaw and trimming their long edges on the router table. I shaped the curves with a drum sander and some careful file work.

The stretchers were roughed out on the bandsaw, and the templates attached with double-faced tape. Then, with a flush-trimming bit, I cut the profiles. Using the same templates, along with a ⅜-in.-dia. template guide on my router base, I routed the ¼-in. grooves in the stretchers (see the second photo from top on the right). To make the routing easier and to give me clean stopping and starting points, I drilled holes at either end of each groove first.

ROUT THE PANEL GROOVES. The author uses shims and a block on the router base to keep the base flush with the legs. The frame is dry-assembled as he makes the cut.

GROOVES IN THE STRETCHERS LIGHTEN THEM VISUALLY. A router, template and ⅜-in.-dia. template guide make the ¼-in.-wide grooves in all four stretchers the same. Double-faced tape holds the template in place.

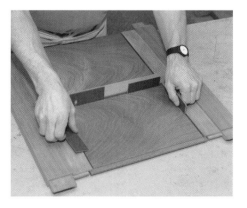

SPACERS ENSURE AN EVEN REVEAL. The author uses ⅛-in.-thick hardboard spacers to set the reveal on end panels. Short sections of ⅛-in.-dia. dowel were later used to pin the panels in place from the inside, at center, top and bottom.

COMPLETING THE SIDE ASSEMBLIES. The last glue-up for the sides mates the four rail tenons and two stretcher tenons with the six leg mortises. Be sure the legs remain flat under clamping pressure. ■

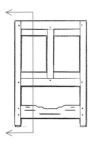

Pieces of varying thicknesses in the end assemblies create shadow lines where the parts meet, giving the ends a sense of depth. The side rails are set back from the face of the legs by ⅛ in. The center stile (not shown) sets back from upper and lower side rails another ⅛ in., and panel rails step back from the center stile another ⅛ in. The panels are ¹⁄₁₆ in. back from the panel rails.

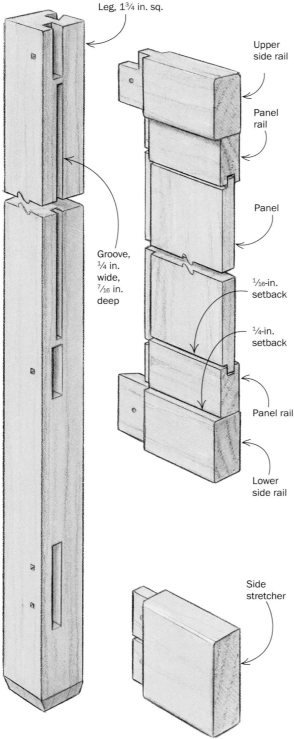

Leg, 1¾ in. sq.

Upper side rail

Panel rail

Groove, ¼ in. wide, ⁷⁄₁₆ in. deep

Panel

¹⁄₁₆-in. setback

¼-in. setback

Panel rail

Lower side rail

Side stretcher

Panels and legs complete the sideboard ends All that remained was to slide in the panels and clamp the legs to the rails. To ensure that the spacing around each panel was the same on all four sides, I used ⅛-in.-thick hardboard spacers (see the third photo from top on p. 71). Then I clamped the assemblies together, taking care to apply pressure evenly across the two side rails and the stretcher (see the bottom photo on p. 71).

I checked the legs to be sure their faces remained flat during glue-up. I also kept the top rails just a tad higher than the tops of the legs. Planing the long grain of the side rails is easier than planing the end grain at the top of the leg.

CONNECTING END ASSEMBLIES WITH RAILS AND STRETCHERS

I tenoned all but one of the rails connecting the two ends, using the same Multi-Router setup I'd used for the mortises and tenons holding the ends together; the one exception was the dovetailed top front rail (see the photo on the facing page).

Preparing for glue-up It was tempting at this point to smear on some glue, throw on the clamps and see how the piece looked. Experience has taught me, however, that preparation is everything.

For starters, my bench was too small and too high. So I built a staging area. I connected four short sawhorses with braces and C-clamps. Then I put a sheet of particleboard on top and shimmed it until it was flat, checking with a pair of large winding sticks.

I dry-assembled the piece exactly as I would glue it up. I figured out where I needed to place all my clamps and cauls and laid them in place. Then, after checking my carcase for square across its faces, I disassembled the piece.

Marking and mortising knife hinges Before gluing up the carcase, I cut the mortises for the knife hinges at either end of the bottom front rail. These mortises can be cut after the carcase has been glued up, but if you wait until then, I guarantee it will become work designed to test your patience and cursing vocabulary.

I also took the opportunity to mortise the hinges at either end of the top front rail at this time. It's a good idea to wait on the mortises for the inner doors (the ones on either side of the center bay) until after the divider panels are in.

I used L-shaped Brusso knife hinges (available from many woodworking suppliers and from Larry and Faye Brusso Co.; 810-674-8458). I spaced them precisely ³⁄₆₄ in. from the legs, using a piece of laminate as a shim. This created a reveal along the hinge stile for the door. I finished marking out the hinges and then disassembled the case.

I routed the hinge mortises to depth with a ³⁄₁₆-in. straight bit, taking care to stay just a little back from the layout lines. I chopped out the front edge and ends of the hinge, laid the hinge in place at a slight angle and marked its back side again with a knife. I carefully pared to this line, checking the fit and paring again until the hinge fit perfectly.

With these hinge mortises completed, I glued up the carcase. I installed the top front rail without glue, just to keep the front legs parallel during glue-up. This piece had to come out as I worked on the case.

DIVIDING THE CARCASE FOR DOORS AND DRAWERS

Despite all precautions and diligence, glue-ups can still be a little crazed, and the results aren't always dead-on. For that reason, I wait to do any interior work in a case piece until after it's glued together. This sideboard is divided into three sections: a center section with web frames for three drawers and two outer sections, each of which has a pair of doors. Separating these sections are two walls, each consisting of a plywood divider panel splined to a solid divider rail below it. Kickers centered on the two divider panels lock them in place.

Melamine spacer simplifies joinery

Stopped sliding dovetails connect the divider rails, which are parallel to the ends of the carcase, to the bottom rails. To index these cuts for my router, I made a spacer that butted up to the legs and was supported by the bottom rail and stretcher. As it turned out, this spacer proved useful again and again in building the carcase. To determine the width of the spacer (15 in., as it turned out), I took the intended opening for the doors and subtracted the distance between the edge of the router sub-base and the center of the bit. Then, to rout the sliding dovetails, I laid the carcase on its face, clamped the spacer in place and routed away. I made two passes for each slot, one with a straight bit to eliminate most of the waste and one with the dovetail bit. Because the carcase is laid out symmetrically, I could use the spacer at both ends.

To size the divider rails, I measured between the front and rear bottom rails right up against the legs, where there was no possibility of bowing. I added ¾ in. for the two dovetails and cut the divider rails to this length. I cut the dovetails on the router table using the same ½-in. dovetail bit I had used to rout the slots. When I was sure the shoulder-to-shoulder length of the divider

WITH THE TOP FRONT RAIL FITTED, THE BASIC STRUCTURE IS COMPLETE. The rail is not glued in place yet. Dovetailed slots still need to be cut for kickers, and knife-hinge mortises must be routed before the rail can be permanently attached.

rail was right, I took a shaving or two off the end of each dovetail with a low-angle block plane so the joints would slide home more easily. Then I glued the divider rails in place, making sure that they were flush with or just slightly above the front and rear bottom rails.

After planing the top and bottom edges of the divider rails flush with the long rails, I concentrated on the divider panels. I made these out of ¾-in. mahogany plywood to avoid shrinkage problems, so my first task was to glue banding on the front edge of each. I made this mahogany strip just as wide as my front rail was thick.

Then the issue was how to attach these panels to the rails. I figured a spline joint was my best bet in terms of strength and ease. I used the same spacer I had used for the dovetails to put a ¼-in. groove dead center into the divider rails (see the photo on p. 76). For the corresponding groove in the edge of the plywood divider panel, I used a handheld plunge router with a secondary fence clamped to its base to keep the cut true.

A spline cut in the top rear rail helps locate the divider panel even before the kicker is installed at the top of the case (see the divider detail on the facing page). I routed this little stopped groove in the top rear rail using the same spacer board, notched the divider panels to fit around the rear rail and routed a groove in the notched section to receive the spline.

Ledger strips support bottom pieces and false bottoms Ledger strips attached to the front, rear, side and divider rails support the ½-in.-thick-plywood bottom panels. I used biscuits to attach the strips to the rails. Then I glued and screwed the bottom panels to the ledger strips from below. The screw holes were plugged later and then sanded flush.

I included a few hidden compartments as a little surprise for the client (see the top right photo on p. 77). When you push down on the rear of the bottom panel, it pivots up and reveals the hidden compartment. I beveled the rear edge of the bottom

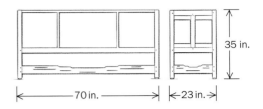

35 in.

70 in. ⟵ 23 in. ⟶

This drawing shows how the major parts of the carcase are joined. The kickers, the front rail and the plywood divider panels should not be glued into the case until dividers have been grooved for the drawer runners. That's covered on pp. 78-85.

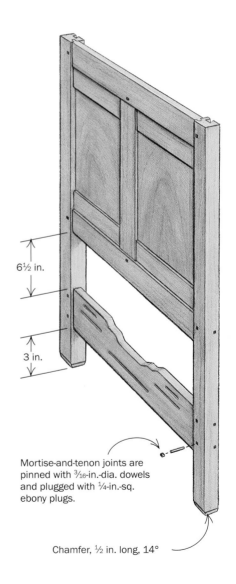

6½ in.

3 in.

Mortise-and-tenon joints are pinned with 3/16-in.-dia. dowels and plugged with ¼-in.-sq. ebony plugs.

Chamfer, ½ in. long, 14°

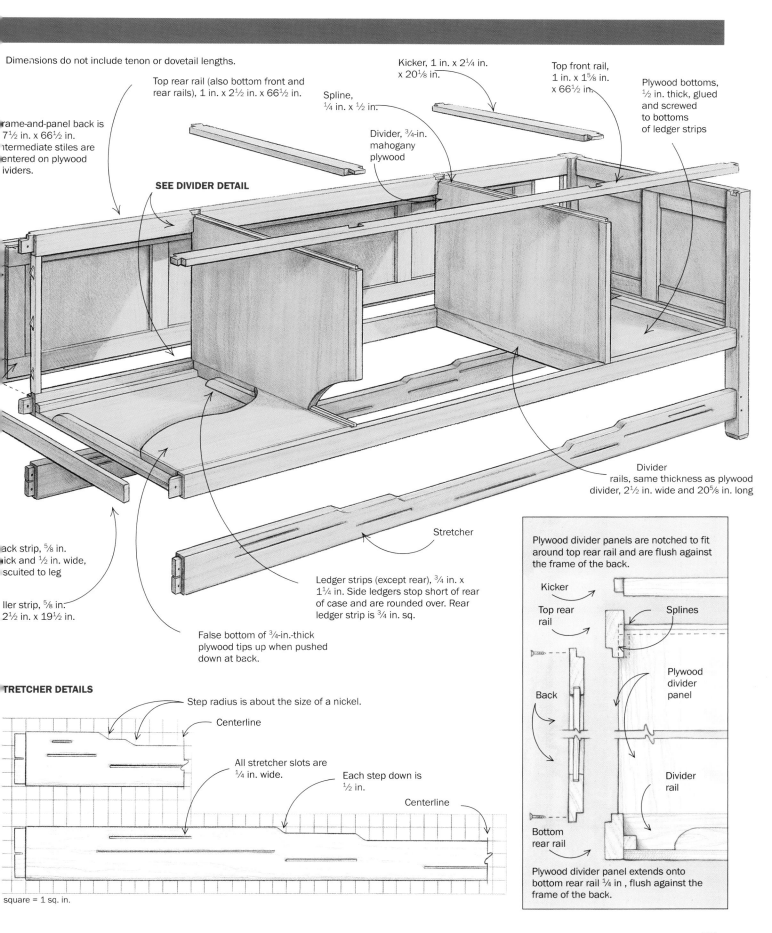

Dimensions do not include tenon or dovetail lengths.

Top rear rail (also bottom front and rear rails), 1 in. x 2½ in. x 66½ in.

Kicker, 1 in. x 2¼ in. x 20⅛ in.

Top front rail, 1 in. x 1⅝ in. x 66½ in.

Plywood bottoms, ½ in. thick, glued and screwed to bottoms of ledger strips

Spline, ¼ in. x ½ in.

Divider, ¾-in. mahogany plywood

Frame-and-panel back is 7½ in. x 66½ in. Intermediate stiles are centered on plywood dividers.

SEE DIVIDER DETAIL

Divider rails, same thickness as plywood divider, 2½ in. wide and 20⅝ in. long

Stretcher

ack strip, ⅝ in. ick and ½ in. wide, scuited to leg

ller strip, ⅝ in. 2½ in. x 19½ in.

False bottom of ¾-in.-thick plywood tips up when pushed down at back.

Ledger strips (except rear), ¾ in. x 1¼ in. Side ledgers stop short of rear of case and are rounded over. Rear ledger strip is ¾ in. sq.

TRETCHER DETAILS

Step radius is about the size of a nickel.

Centerline

All stretcher slots are ¼ in. wide.

Each step down is ½ in.

Centerline

square = 1 sq. in.

Plywood divider panels are notched to fit around top rear rail and are flush against the frame of the back.

Kicker

Top rear rail

Splines

Back

Plywood divider panel

Bottom rear rail

Divider rail

Plywood divider panel extends onto bottom rear rail ¼ in , flush against the frame of the back.

A jig for centering grooves and dovetails

DIVIDER RAILS ARE GROOVED FOR SPLINES. Splines connect the rails to plywood dividers. The same spacer used to rout the dovetails for the divider rails is used here. ■

panel just like a door so it wouldn't bind. At the same time, I kept the fit of the panel very snug so it wouldn't be obvious. Just in case it was a little too snug, I drilled a small access hole through the front ledger strip, so a short length of ⅛-in.-dia. rod could be used to push the false bottom up from below.

Kickers tie case together and prevent top drawer from dropping The kickers had to be cut before I could cut the divider panels to their finished height. I attached the kickers to the top rails with large dovetails. I cut the slots with a router, using a pair of spacers (one for each side of the slot) similar to the one I'd used for the divider rails. Because the top front rail is flush with the back of the front leg, there's no leg edge for the spacer. To get around this, I just set a ⅝-in.-thick block against the inside of the frame instead.

I cut the kickers to length, notched their shoulder locations on the tablesaw and

checked to see that the length was right. Then I transferred the dovetail layout from the slots in the top rails, cut the dovetails by hand and fitted them to the slots.

Divider panels fit between divider rails and kickers I measured and cut the divider panels to fit between the kickers and divider rails. The kicker and the top of the panel were grooved for the same ¼-in.-wide spline I used on the panel bottom. My first spacer centers the groove in line with the panel and divider rail. But because the router base runs into the rear top rail, I couldn't finish this cut with the kicker in the carcase. So I used the router table.

I clamped the divider panels in place vertically to the kickers and divider rails to check the drawer openings. I made sure they were parallel from front to back. Any slight adjusting can be done by cutting the grooves in the panel a bit wider so the plywood can be moved, shimming the spline to one side or the other. Once I'd positioned

THE CASE IS BUILT. With the two end assemblies connected and the case divided into its three main sections, the carcase is ready for doors and drawers (left). The case includes two hidden compartments (above).

the dividers exactly where I wanted them, I clamped them in place and pencil-marked their positions. Then I laid out the remaining knife-hinge mortises.

Unfortunately, I had glued in the rail splines to make it easier to fit the dividers. This prevented the router base from riding the rails to rout the mortises for the knife hinges. After shrieking with disgust over my lack of foresight, I realized there was a simple way to correct this problem that was actually an improvement. I made a little platform out of some ¼-in.-thick medium-density fiberboard (MDF), clamping it in place around each mortise location. These boards were just higher than the spline and provided the router base with solid support.

MAKING AND FITTING THE BACK

The back of this sideboard was fitted with a frame-and-panel back. The top and bottom rear rails were rabbeted to receive the panel. Rather than rabbeting the legs and weakening them, I glued strips to the rear legs to provide support for the back. If by some fluke of nature, the opening for the back is not perfectly square, cut your rails and stiles to the largest dimension and trim the frame after it's glued up.

For ease of construction, I used stub tenons for this frame. I made the mortises for these tenons slightly deeper than the panel grooves, though, so the center stiles wouldn't be hard to locate during glue-up. Be sure when gluing up that the end stiles line up flush or are just proud of the rail ends. Again, it's easier to plane long grain than end grain. The panels were sanded and finished before gluing. After the glue had cured, I pinned all the joints with ¼-in. dowels and drilled countersunk holes for the screws that hold the back in place.

Then I fit the fraame to its opening and rabbeted it so it would be flush with the top and bottom rails. Once fit, the back was set aside in a safe place.

GARY ROGOWSKI

Building an Arts-and-Crafts Sideboard (Part II)

I've seen many a piece of furniture that looked great from across a room but fell short on closer inspection. Often, it's something as simple as a drawer binding in its opening or a pair of doors that aren't aligned properly. That's why building and

fitting these parts carefully is every bit as important to a piece of furniture as making a sturdy case.

The previous section (pp. 68-77) covered carcase construction for the Arts-and-Crafts style sideboard in the photo at

right. That section ends with the mahogany case pieces made and mostly glued up. Now it's time for those all important details: adding web frames to support the three drawers and then building and installing both drawers and doors.

BUILDING WEB FRAMES FOR THE DRAWERS

On many case pieces, the front rail of a web frame—also called a drawer divider—is visible on the outside of the case. On this sideboard, however, I kept the dividers hidden behind the drawer fronts to act as drawer stops. One other benefit of keeping the dividers hidden is that the front of the sideboard has a cleaner, less cluttered look.

All three web frames are made of western maple. The side rails of the upper two frames have tongues that are glued into stopped grooves in the plywood dividers (see the drawing on p. 81).

The side rails are joined to the front web-frame rails with stub tenons ⅜ in. thick and ¼ in. long. The front rails are joined to the plywood dividers with stub tenons of the same size. Web-frame joinery was done on the tablesaw and router table (see the top photo at right). No matter how you do it, make sure the shoulder-to-shoulder lengths of the front rails are all exactly the same. Otherwise, the plywood dividers won't be straight when the rails are in place, altering the size of the drawer openings and making drawer fitting much more difficult.

The bottom drawer also needs a web frame, but I was concerned that if I used the same joinery as I had for the upper two web frames, the grooves would be too close to the spline joints connecting the dividers and divider rails. Grooves located this close to each other would have compromised both joints.

My solution was to use 1½-in.-wide stock for the front and side rails of the bottom web frame (this increased the glue surface area), biscuit the side rails to the divider rails and rabbet the front web-frame rail over the front rail of the carcase (see the drawing on p. 81). The side rails, or

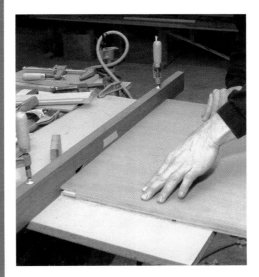

ROUT WEB FRAME GROOVES IN DIVIDERS. Start and stop marks are penciled on the masking tape on the router-table fence and on the divider itself. Dividers get two grooves on their inside faces for the top two web frames.

GLUE DIVIDER TO DIVIDER RAIL. Once the grooves for the web frames have been routed, the dividers can be glued into the case. Make sure the front of the dividers are flush with the outer face of the lower front rail (below). ■

DUST PANEL IS SUPPORTED ON ALL FOUR SIDES. Because the ⅛-in.-thick plywood panel sagged when he first slid it home, the author added a rear rail to the web frame.

runners, were simply butted to the backs of the front rails. After all the web-frame rails were fitted, I planed their tops and bottoms flush to one another and cut grooves for the dust panels.

GLUE IN DIVIDERS, TOP RAIL AND KICKERS

The next step was to finish assembling the case. I glued the dividers to the divider rails (see the photo on p. 79). I glued in one at a time and used the front bottom web-frame rail as a spacer between the plywood dividers when gluing in the second one. Dry-clamping the top front carcase rail and kickers to the dividers kept the drawer openings precisely aligned during assembly. After both dividers were in, I glued the top rail and then the kickers in place.

I set the web frames back in place, and checked them for twist using a pair of winding sticks. I pre-finished the web-frame rails with three coats of shellac, being careful to keep it off the joinery. Then I glued all the web-frame rails in place.

I cut dust panels out of ⅛-in.-thick mahogany plywood, but when I slid them in place, they sagged too much for my liking. To remedy this, I added rear rails to the web frames, using ⅛-in.-thick splines to

attach them to the side rails (see the photo at left). I left these rear web-frame rails unglued until after the drawers had been fitted, so I would have a better view of the drawers while working on them.

MAKE DOORS AND DRAWERS OF QUARTERSAWN STOCK

I used quartersawn mahogany for the drawer faces and doors for two reasons: the grain pattern of quartersawn stock is less flashy than flatsawn (it works better as a background for inlay), and quartersawn shrinks less than flatsawn.

I had a problem at first with the quartersawn mahogany, though. I would get tearout every time that I sent it through the planer because the grain was interlocked. I'd heard that dampening wood reduces tearout, so I gave it a shot. It worked beautifully. Just before sending a board through the planer, I dampened (not soaked) its face with a rag. This softened the fibers just enough that they could be cut cleanly with no tearout.

I was concerned about finding a secondary wood for the drawer sides that would move at the same rate as the mahogany. I wanted a wood that was also quartersawn but wore better than the mahogany. I was fortunate to stumble across some quartered sycamore that was glorious to look at and tough enough for the job. Using the formula in Bruce Hoadley's book *Understanding Wood* (The Taunton Press, 2000), I compared the shrinkage rates of mahogany and sycamore. I found that in a board 8 in. wide—the width of my widest drawer—there was less than 1⁄32 in. of difference in shrinkage between the two species. I had found the right wood for my drawer sides. And sycamore is a beautiful contrast to the mahogany.

I resawed the sycamore to just over ½ in. thick, stickered it for a few days and then milled it to ⅜ in. thick. I kept the drawer sides thin to reduce the weight.

Drawers are dovetailed I don't cut half-blind dovetails every day, so I swept the

Each web frame consists of a divider, or front rail, a pair of runners and a rear rail. The pieces are grooved for a dust panel. The two top frames are dadoed into the divider panels. The bottom frame is joined to the carcase with biscuits.

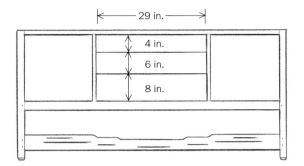

SECTION THROUGH CARCASE WITH PLYWOOD DIVIDER PANEL REMOVED

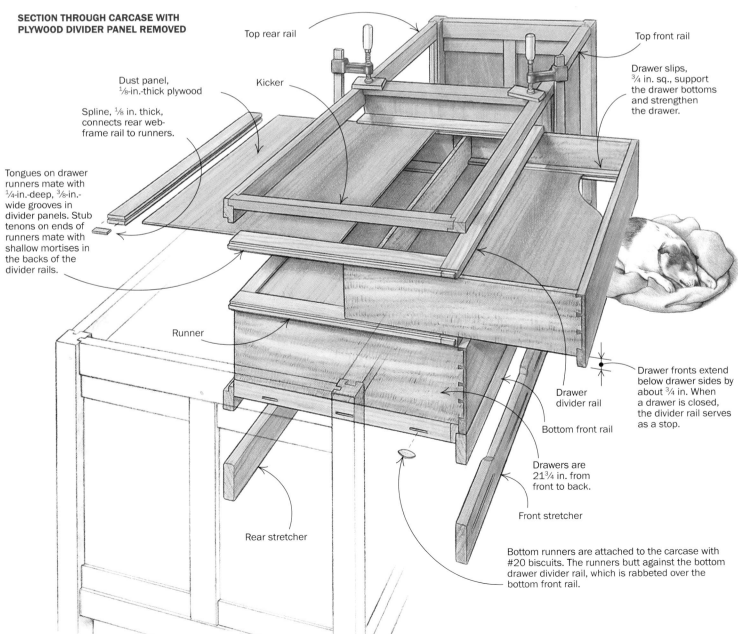

Top rear rail

Kicker

Top front rail

Dust panel, ⅛-in.-thick plywood

Spline, ⅛ in. thick, connects rear web-frame rail to runners.

Tongues on drawer runners mate with ¼-in.-deep, ⅜-in.-wide grooves in divider panels. Stub tenons on ends of runners mate with shallow mortises in the backs of the divider rails.

Drawer slips, ¾ in. sq., support the drawer bottoms and strengthen the drawer.

Runner

Rear stretcher

Drawer divider rail

Bottom front rail

Front stretcher

Drawer fronts extend below drawer sides by about ¾ in. When a drawer is closed, the divider rail serves as a stop.

Drawers are 21¾ in. from front to back.

Bottom runners are attached to the carcase with #20 biscuits. The runners butt against the bottom drawer divider rail, which is rabbeted over the bottom front rail.

Breadboard ends ⅛ in. thicker than door panels keep the doors flat. Quartersawn stock ensures a minimum of movement across the door panels.

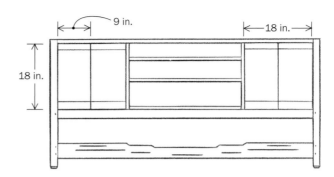

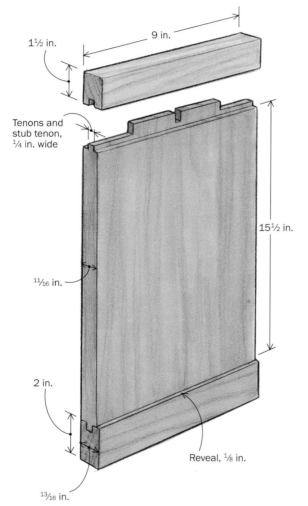

1½ in.

9 in.

Tenons and stub tenon, ¼ in. wide

15½ in.

11⁄16 in.

2 in.

Reveal, ⅛ in.

13⁄16 in.

SHIMS OF PLASTIC LAMINATE keep the reveal around the door consistent.

TAP THE SCREW HOLE with a steel screw, and then replace it with the softer brass screw.

shop floor twice (okay, three times) before getting down to business. But once I started cutting them, things went smoothly. When I cut dovetails for drawers, I lay out the joints so the drawer sides are slightly proud of the tightly fitted drawer fronts when the parts are glued together. This results in easier planing and a better final fit.

I joined the drawer backs to the sides with sliding dovetails (the backs sit on the drawer bottoms). I roughed out the slots in the sides on a tablesaw and then routed them to finished size on a router table. The dovetails on the ends of the backs were cut on the router table using the same bit and height setting used for the slots. Rather than resetting the fence if the joint doesn't quite fit, take a pass with a handplane across the face of the board, and then run it by the bit again. Taking one light pass off the end grain of the dovetail also helps ease the fit.

I added drawer slips to the inside bottom edges of the drawer sides to give the edge of the drawer more bearing surface (see the drawing on p. 81). This helps prevent wear in the drawer runners. Drawer slips also are grooved for the drawer bottoms. This is stronger than grooving the ⅜-in.-thick drawer sides. Slips are notched to fit around the drawer backs.

I glued the half-blind dovetails at the front of the drawers with the back set in dry to keep the drawer square. I checked diagonal measurements inside the drawers to make sure they were the same and used a clamp to adjust the drawers square where necessary. After the glue had set, I carefully removed the backs, checked and trimmed the height of the drawer sides to fit their openings. Then I glued the backs in place, using scrap plywood in the drawer grooves to keep the back from going down too far in the dovetailed slot.

A feeler gauge helps fit the drawers

If the drawers go together square, half the battle is over. Fitting each drawer to its opening will be much easier. I started planing at the rear of the drawer sides and worked my way forward, fitting the drawers until they

slid home smoothly. I used a long, very thin feeler gauge (available from most auto-parts stores) to let me know where a drawer was hung up. Once all the drawers were fitted, I trimmed the top and bottom edges of each of the drawer fronts to get even reveals between them all. I planed the drawer faces flush to each other last.

One final touch for the top drawer in this sideboard was to glue in a divider and a velvet bottom to protect the silverware that would likely be put in it. I glued the velvet to a thin piece of cardboard using a can of aerosol spray mount (you can buy it at art-supply stores). You'll want to use a respirator when using this stuff. Then I trimmed off the excess fabric around the edges and glued the cardboard to the plywood drawer bottom. Make sure the groove for the drawer bottom is wide enough to accommodate the extra thickness of the cardboard and velvet.

A shaped divider slides into dadoes cut in the front and back of the top drawer. I screwed the drawer bottom to the divider from below to prevent the bottom from sagging under the weight of silverware.

Breadboard ends keep door panels flat

Because the door openings are 18 in. sq., I thought two doors for each side would look better than one. Rather than using a traditional frame-and-panel construction, I designed the doors as panels with breadboard ends (see the drawing on p. 82). This helps reinforce the strong horizontal lines of this sideboard and keeps the front from looking cluttered. The breadboard ends keep the panels flat yet still allow for movement, and the quartersawn mahogany minimizes the amount of shrinkage. The breadboard ends are ⅛ in. thicker than the panels to add a shadow line to the front of the sideboard.

When fitting the joints, make sure that the breadboard ends slide onto the panels with just hand pressure. Otherwise, the ends may split.

To keep the breadboard ends tight against the panels, I planed a slight concavity along their lengths. When I glued the

BULLET CATCH PILOT HOLES are enlarged separately. Using a portable drill with a masking tape stop on the bit, the author enlarges the catch and stop holes and drills them to depth. The doors should be supported when the catch holes are being enlarged.

DOOR CATCHES MUST BE ALIGNED PERFECTLY. Bullet catches won't work unless the catch and strike plate line up precisely, so the author drills through the top rail and into the door to locate the holes for both parts simultaneously. The guide block clamped to the top rail prevents the drill bit from wandering.

ends in place, I used a clamp to draw in their centers. This forces the ends in tight.

One of the other advantages of dimensioning the breadboard ends ⅛ in. thicker than the door panels, besides the shadow line, is that you can hammer against this lip to disassemble the doors when you're fitting them. I used a block of scrap and held my hammer flat to the panel. The disadvantage is that you can't plane the face of the door to make it flush with its neighbor—the breadboard end gets in the way. To simplify things, I disassembled the doors and cleaned up the ends and panels individually before gluing each assembly together. Then I glued only the center 2 in. to 3 in. of the tenon and clamped the breadboard ends to the panel.

Laminate shims help set reveal Because door rails should line up horizontally, whatever you do to the rail on one door, you need to do to the corresponding rail on the other door. I started by fitting the bottom rail and hinge side of one door to the opening. Using pieces of laminate to set the reveal, I handplaned the bottom and hinge edges of the door until the reveal was consistent. Then I mortised the door for the bottom knife hinge.

With the bottom hinge in place (but not screwed in), I trimmed the door's top rail until its reveal was consistent with the bottom and hinge side reveals. Then I mortised for the top hinge. I repeated these steps for the second door. Something to keep in mind is that if the doors don't align across their faces, you can alter that alignment somewhat by moving a hinge mortise slightly in or out. Make any adjustments on the bottom rail hinge mortises where they won't be noticeable.

Before any final fitting of the door reveals, I set steel screws into the hinges. I used a Vix bit, which is self-centering, to set the screw hole center. Then I drilled the hole to depth, put some wax on a steel screw and drove it home. This cut the

threads for the hole and eliminated the risk of snapping off the head of one of the softer brass screws.

When both doors were hinged and all screws had been driven home, I checked the reveal between the two doors (see the top photo on p. 82) and planed as necessary to make this reveal the same as the others. Also, I planed a slight bevel along their mating edges so the doors would have room to open. Then I replaced the steel screws with the brass ones that came with the hinges.

Bullet catches give a positive stop Bullet catches make a satisfying thunk when they engage, but they have to be placed with bull's-eye accuracy if they are to work at all. I wedged the doors firmly in place with scrap; then I drilled down through a guide block, through the top front rail, through the scrap and into each door with a $\frac{3}{16}$-in.-dia. bit (see the photo at left on p. 84). Drilling both holes at once guaranteed that mating pieces of the catch would be aligned.

Once I'd established the location of the holes with the $\frac{3}{16}$-in.-bit, I used a series of progressively larger twist drill bits to enlarge the holes to ¼ in. I enlarged the holes in the door and rail separately, drilling up into the front rail and down into the edge of the door. I supported the doors when drilling the holes to avoid putting a lot of shear on the hinge screws. I used masking tape stops on the bits to let me know when I was at depth. I set the bullet catch and strike plate into their holes with a dab of epoxy and used a clamp and a wooden caul to pull them home. I applied clamping pressure very gradually because both catch and strike plate tended to resist the clamping force at first and then give way all of a sudden.

I attached door stops to the insides of the door openings with brass screws. Leather pads were set into shallow mortises in the stops with barge cement.

Projects & Techniques

Building an Arts-and-Crafts Sideboard (Part III)

Details in a handmade piece of furniture are what make it sing, and where a furnituremaker can really have fun. In some ways, this mahogany sideboard looks as if it could have been designed by Charles and Henry Greene in the early 1900s. I relied on the inlay of ebony and carved yellow heart to make this design my own.

The last two sections (pp. 68-85) covered construction of the carcase, the web frames, which support the drawers, and the doors. What's left is the top, back rail, drawer pulls and door handles, and, finally, the inlay across the front of the case. Although each of these remaining parts gave me some chance to experiment with design, I especially looked forward to the carved inlay that would simulate ginkgo leaves blowing across the face of the finished sideboard.

A BREADBOARD TOP STAYS FLAT BUT ALLOWS SEASONAL MOVEMENT

To keep the top flat, I used breadboard ends, which prevent the top from cupping yet still allow it to move across its width as humidity changes. The breadboard ends were dimensioned $\frac{1}{16}$ in. thicker than the top and a little longer than the top is wide, adding shadow lines. The top and breadboard ends are flush on the bottom.

To join the breadboard ends and top, I used four mortises and tenons at each end,

along with a full-length groove in the ends and a mating tongue at either end of the top (see the drawing on pp. 88-89).

The mortises and grooves in the breadboard ends were cut on the router table. The tenons and tongue across the ends of the top, both $\frac{1}{4}$ in. thick, were cut with a hand-held plunge router after being defined by sawkerfs. Remember that any trimming to fit must be from the top cheek of the tenon so the bottoms of the breadboard ends and top remain flush. When the tenons were finally seated, I pulled the two end pieces off and planed a slight belly along their inside edges. This spring joint ensures that the joints between top and ends remain tight.

Once the joinery was cut and fitted, I eased all exposed edges on the top and ends, except for those where the ends meet the top. I finish-planed and then wet-sanded before I glued on the ends. This work is easy now, but a real pain later on.

PINS AND PLUGS FINISH TOP, FUNCTIONALLY AND DECORATIVELY

Because the top has to be able to move across its width, I couldn't glue all four tenons on each end into their respective mortises. Instead, I glued just the center two tenons and used short sections of dowel to pin all the tenons. The outer two

tenons have slotted pin holes so the top can move. I plugged all four holes at each end with squared ebony plugs.

With the top and breadboard ends apart, I drilled the ¼-in.-dia. plug holes (about ¼ in. deep) into the ends and then squared them. These holes do not go into the mor-

tise. Next I drilled ³⁄₁₆-in.-dia. pin holes (centered on the ¼-in. holes) through the mortises and just into the bottom half of the breadboard ends. Then I dry-clamped the top and ends together and marked the pin locations on the tenons. I pulled the ends off, drilled the holes in the two center

INLAY IS THE FINISHING TOUCH. Carved inlay in the shape of ginkgo leaves help put the author's stamp on this mahogany sideboard. Leaves were carved and positioned to look as if they were scattered across the doors by the wind.

Sideboard Top and Back Rail

Breadboard ends keep the top flat and create shadow lines for visual interest. The ends are pinned and plugged. The back rail is attached to the top rear rail of the carcase with a pair of brackets that are notched to fit around the overhang of the top.

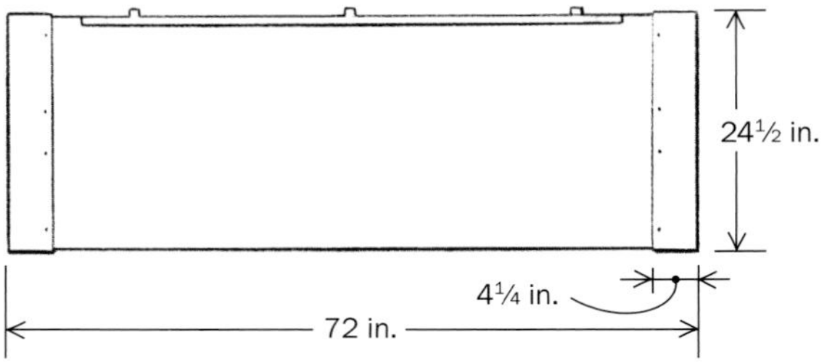

24½ in.
4¼ in.
72 in.

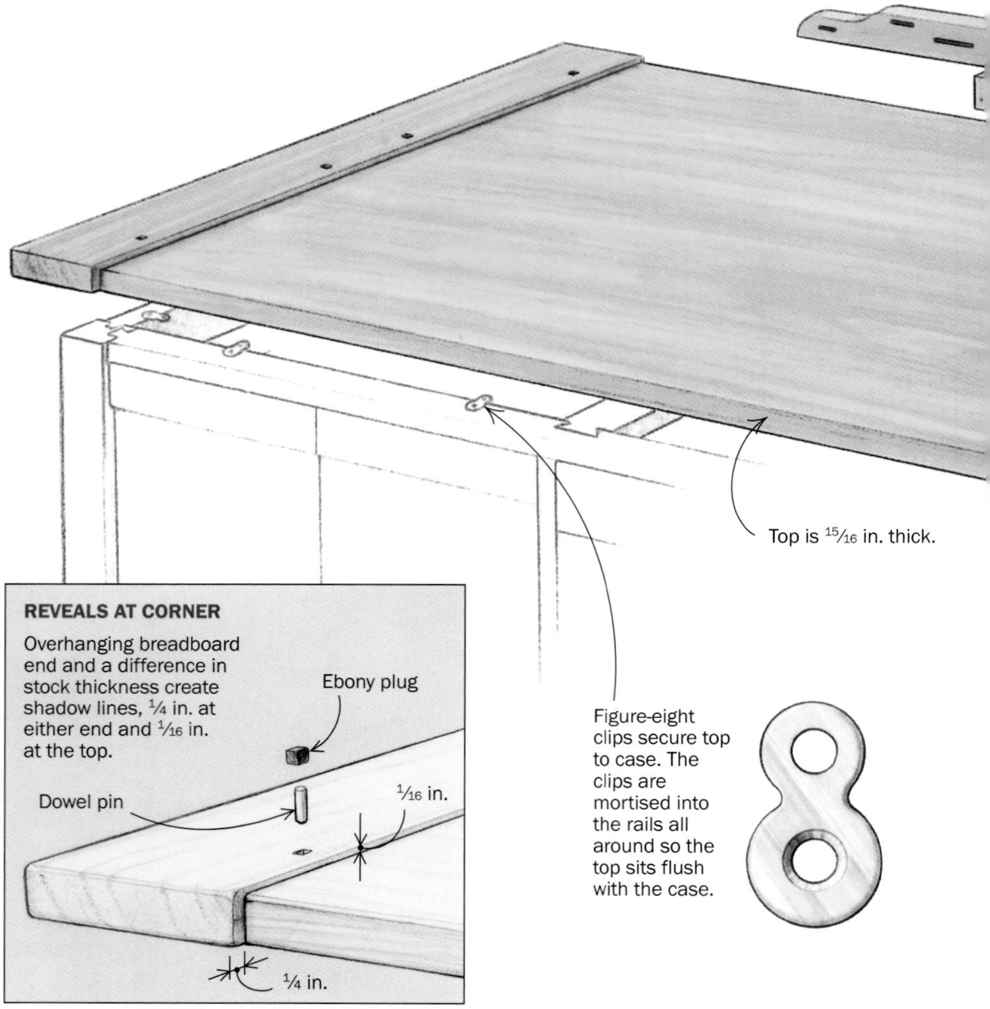

Top is 15/16 in. thick.
REVEALS AT CORNER
Overhanging breadboard end and a difference in stock thickness create shadow lines, ¼ in. at either end and 1/16 in. at the top.
Ebony plug
Dowel pin
1/16 in.
¼ in.
Figure-eight clips secure top to case. The clips are mortised into the rails all around so the top sits flush with the case.

tenons at each end and routed ½-in.-long slots in the outer tenons.

I glued and clamped the breadboard ends to the top next (see the left photo on p. 90). When you glue the ends on, make sure you have the same reveal at both edges of the top and that the ends pull in at their centers. Have long clamps ready to apply pressure on both sides of the top, and make sure the ends don't deflect under clamping pressure. If you don't have long enough clamps, threaded couplers can connect lengths of pipe clamp.

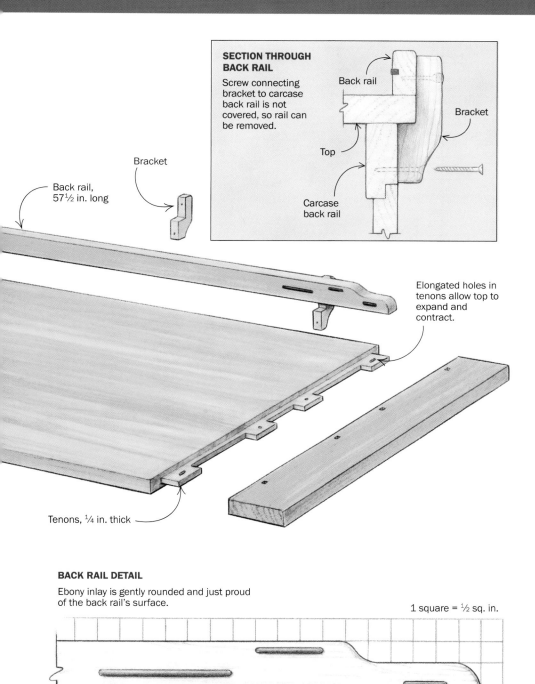

SECTION THROUGH BACK RAIL

Screw connecting bracket to carcase back rail is not covered, so rail can be removed.

Back rail

Bracket

Top

Carcase back rail

Bracket

Back rail, 57½ in. long

Elongated holes in tenons allow top to expand and contract.

Tenons, ¼ in. thick

BACK RAIL DETAIL

Ebony inlay is gently rounded and just proud of the back rail's surface.

1 square = ½ sq. in.

I pinned the four mortise-and-tenon joints at each end of the top with short sections of ³⁄₁₆-in.-dia. dowel, driving them home with a piece of brass rod (see the center photo on p. 90). Then I tapered one end of each of the ¼-in.-sq. ebony plugs to ease their entry into the squared holes in the breadboard ends. I hammered these home, stopping when I could hear that they were fully seated (see the far right photo on p. 90).

This sideboard called for a soft, rounded look, so I domed the plugs using a chisel and sandpaper. A scrap of plastic laminate prevented damage to the breadboard ends as I pared down the ebony plugs to within $\frac{1}{16}$ in. of the surface. I finished doming the plugs with 180-grit sandpaper, stopping when I could run my finger over a plug without catching an edge.

I attached the top to the carcase with 20 figure-eight clips. I used a ¾-in.-dia. straight bit in a plunge router to cut the recesses in the top rails for the clips. Because the figure-eights can pivot, the top is free to expand and contract.

A low back rail doesn't overwhelm the case I had originally designed the back rail as a 5-in.-high plate rail with cutouts similar to those in the stretchers. But later, something told me that such a tall back rail wasn't quite right. So I started mocking up other possibilities on cardboard, using a marker to indicate inlay. I arrived at a rail just 1½ in. high and inlaid with strips of ebony. The effect is lighter and more graceful than what I had intended.

I routed ⅛-in.-wide grooves in the back rail for the inlay, using support pieces on either side of the rail to keep the router base steady. To fit the inlay, I planed the ebony to thickness, sanded one end round to fit and then cut the other end close to length. I snuck up on a fit by sanding a little off the other end, checking and repeating until it just fit the groove. Once I'd glued the ebony in place, I domed its top to match the plugs in the top and elsewhere on the sideboard.

To attach the back rail, I glued, screwed and plugged brackets to it from behind, notching them to fit around the overhang of the top (see the drawing on p. 89). The brackets are screwed to the back of the carcase. To ensure accuracy, I attached the brackets with the back rail in place.

HANDLES ARE DESIGNED AFTER THE PIECE IS BUILT

I never design handles for a piece of furniture until it's built. It's impossible to know what will look right until then. I started

■ Pinned joints

  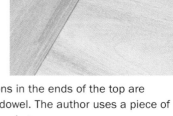

GLUE ONLY THE CENTER. The center two mortise-and-tenon joints are glued. The other two are pinned through elongated holes but assembled without glue so the top can move with seasonal changes in humidity.

JOINTS ARE PINNED AND THEN PLUGGED. Tenons in the ends of the top are pinned in place with short sections of ³⁄₁₆-in.-dia. dowel. The author uses a piece of brass rod to set the pins before adding the ebony plugs.

Both pulls and handles are made of mahogany with ebony inlay. The ebony is pared down and gently rounded until it's just proud of the mahogany.

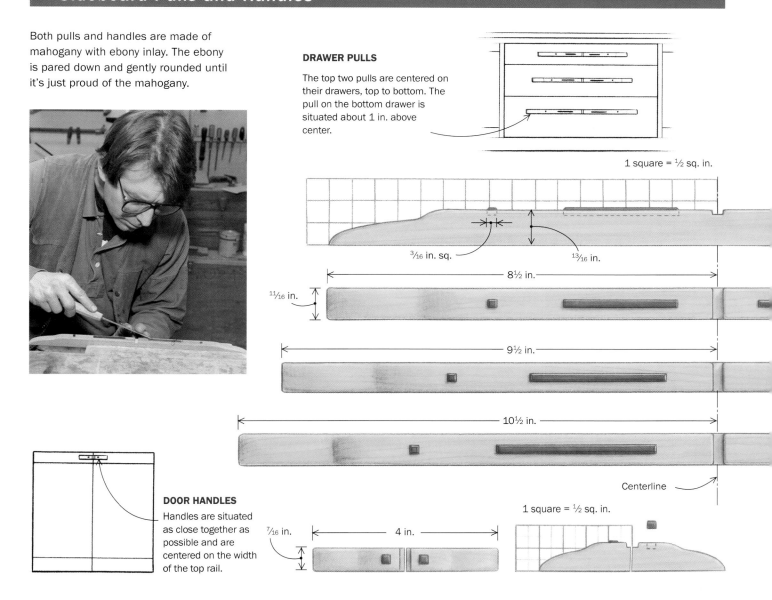

DRAWER PULLS

The top two pulls are centered on their drawers, top to bottom. The pull on the bottom drawer is situated about 1 in. above center.

1 square = ½ sq. in.

³⁄₁₆ in. sq.

¹³⁄₁₆ in.

8½ in.

¹¹⁄₁₆ in.

9½ in.

10½ in.

Centerline

1 square = ½ sq. in.

DOOR HANDLES

Handles are situated as close together as possible and are centered on the width of the top rail.

⁷⁄₁₆ in.

4 in.

with a stylized ginkgo-leaf shape for the door handles. It looked great there, but it didn't work as a drawer pull—it wasn't enough for the huge expanse of drawer face.

I mocked up longer pulls so they would be more prominent. I kept playing with the proportions of the pulls until they felt right both visually and in my hands. I settled on long mahogany pulls with a pattern of ebony inlay in them (see the drawing above). For the door handles, I shortened the pulls and included one square of ebony. The undersides of the pulls are slightly coved to provide a better grip.

Door handles are placed as close to each other as possible, centered in the width of each top door rail. Locating the drawer pulls took a bit more head scratching. Both pulls and inlay increase in length from top to bottom. I wanted them to line up on a diagonal, with each of the pulls centered on the width of the drawer, but when I tried that, it just didn't look right. I ended up keeping the top two pulls centered in the drawer faces, but I positioned the bottom pull nearly 1 in. above center.

■ Carving the leaves

A GUST OF WIND SENDS THE LEAVES FLYING. The author sought a natural looking display of leaves blowing across the front of the sideboard. He taped real leaves on the doors as he worked toward a final design.

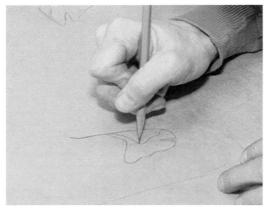

TRACE, THEN CUT. The author transfers a drawing to cardboard with carbon paper (left). Patterns are used to trace leaves on the inlay before they are cut (above).

SHAPE THE LEAVES, AND BEVEL THEIR EDGES. A spindle sander does the job quickly (left), but the author needs a knife to get into tight corners. He scribes a leaf on a door (above).

(continued on p. 94)

ROUT OUT MOST OF THE WASTE; then pare to the line. After routing as close to the line as he dares, the author finishes the job with carving gouges, cutting straight down or slightly undercutting.

PRESS, TAP AND THEN CLAMP THE INLAY. The author used a caul to distribute clamping pressure evenly across the inlay.

DETAIL IS CARVED IN. The author creates depth and motion in the leaves through his use of line and texture.

THE ILLUSION OF DEPTH. With just ³⁄₃₂ in. of leaf above the surface of the door, every cut counts when carving. Deeply incised cuts where the leaves fold or curl create shadow lines that suggest depth. Gentle, flowing curves give the leaves an organic feel. ∎

GINKGO LEAVES SWEPT BY THE WIND

This inlay work was the detail I was most excited about. It was a chance to break away from the Greene and Greene mold. What I hoped to create was a natural-looking display of ginkgo leaves, as if a gust of wind had just blown a small pile of them across the front of the sideboard.

I got the patterns for my carved leaves from real ginkgo leaves I'd collected (like the one on the facing page). I began by drawing these shapes until I felt I had a sense of what the leaf looked like, whether flat or curled, falling or tumbling in a breeze. Because the leaves were brittle, I also made up some cardboard versions, which I folded and rolled to mimic real leaves. Then I started to draw various leaf shapes on large sheets of brown paper where I had drawn the outline of the doors.

When I liked a leaf, I traced its shape onto cardboard using carbon paper and a pencil and cut out the pattern (see the far left photo on the facing page). Then I played with the position of each leaf. A yellow marking pen brightened the cardboard enough to give it some life. I began designing with the leaf patterns by applying them to the real doors with double-faced tape.

Inlay is sawn, shaped and beveled The wood I chose for the inlay was yellow heart. This South American wood is valued for its consistent yellow color and is often used in parquet flooring and, surprisingly, fabric dye. It was perfect for the autumn yellow of my ginkgo leaves.

I used quartersawn material to minimize wood movement and resawed it into pieces 3/16 in. thick. The leaf pattern was marked on the yellow heart so the grain followed the direction of the stem. This way, I wouldn't have to worry about a stem breaking off because of short grain.

I cut the leaves on a bandsaw and scrollsaw, then shaped and beveled them slightly, using a sanding drum (see the top right and bottom left photos on the facing page). Any edges I couldn't reach with the sanding drum were shaped and beveled with a knife.

RECESS FOR INLAY IS ROUTED, THEN REFINED WITH CARVING TOOLS

The next step was to transfer the leaf patterns to the door. I placed each piece of inlay on the door in position, marking its shape with a scratch awl and with a thin knife in very tight spots (see the bottom right photo on p. 92). Accuracy at this point is critical. A slip of the knife can create nasty marks on the door's surface, and a slip of the inlay will result in an inaccurate pattern that's nearly impossible to fix. Take your time, keep a firm grip on the inlay and make sure the entire perimeter of the leaf is marked before you lift it off the door. I darkened the incised line with a soft pencil—it's much easier to see than a knife line when you're routing.

To create the recess, I used a 3/16-in.-dia. straight bit in a fixed-base router and set its depth of cut at 3/32 in. I attached spacer strips to the door with double-faced tape to bring the router base up to the level of the door rails. Then, after a deep breath, I began routing out the inlay pattern (see the top left photo on p. 94). I started at the center of each pattern and gradually worked my way out to the edges. Because the bit pulls itself into the cut when routing clockwise, I cut in the opposite direction to maintain control.

For the leaf stems, I used a 1/16-in.-dia. straight bit; then I switched to a shopmade, 1/32-in.-wide chisel. I put a hollow grind on its edge, honed it razor sharp and used it to finish cutting the stem recesses to depth.

After routing, I trimmed the walls of each recess with carving tools, trying to keep them straight or just slightly undercut (see the top right photo on p. 94).

Then I began fitting each leaf. I used carving tools and a sanding drum. I checked the fit often—until the leaf fit almost all the way down into its ground. If a leaf sticks in its recess, lever it out with the edge of a #1 gouge or a skew chisel.

When I was comfortable with the fit of a leaf, I spread a little glue in the recess, pressed the leaf into place and then tapped it so it was well-seated (see the center photo on p. 94). Then I put a caul over the leaf and another under the door and clamped the inlay until it would go no farther. There was a considerable amount of glue squeeze-out, so I pulled my clamps after three hours and cleaned up the excess.

When the glue had cured, I carved in the wind. Here was a chance to play with the shape and texture. I spent about an hour working on each leaf with #3 and #5 gouges, carving in the gentle undulations and curves that you see in falling leaves. Then I lightly trimmed each leaf edge with a #1 skew chisel to make them friendly to the touch. Do this with a carving tool, not sandpaper. Sandpaper will smear the details and leave a soft, unsatisfying edge. After each leaf had been carved, I burnished its surface with a piece of burlap.

FINISHING THE SIDEBOARD: SHELLAC INSIDE, VARNISH OUTSIDE

For all the interior surfaces of this cabinet, I used a 1½-lb. cut of dewaxed super blond shellac (a proportion of 1½ lb. of shellac flakes to a gallon of denatured alcohol) that I mixed myself. I added a few drops of jasmine oil (available in many health-food stores) to this mixture to give it a pleasant scent. This finish is easy to apply, dries quickly and has a much nicer aroma than lacquer, varnish or oil. The drawers were shellacked inside and out except for their faces. I also waxed the drawer sides and web frames after the shellac had dried.

For the exterior of the sideboard, I used a product called ProFin manufactured by Daly's (for a distributor, call 800-735-7019). It's a wiping varnish that's easy to apply, and it gives a lustrous finish in three coats. I used the gloss version. I tried to make sure that all the dust in my shop had settled before applying the final coat. I wanted to avoid having to rub out that last coat with anything but a polishing cloth.

THE CARCASE. On pp. 68-77, Gary Rogowski described the construction of this sideboard's carcase, including its two interior divider panels and the back.

DRAWERS AND DOORS. Final carcase glue-ups, construction of the web frames, and drawers and doors are described on pp. 78-85.

THE FINISHED PIECE. The sideboard is complete. Gary and Buck get ready to head home after finishing another successful project. ■

JOHN McALEVEY

A Blanket Chest with Legs

I have always liked designing and making sideboards, chests of drawers and blanket chests. It is very satisfying to make a basic box that will contain and store the things that we use in our everyday lives. And when it works, the result can be as beautiful as it is useful. It's even more satisfying when you can transform a basic box into something with depth, dimension and visual power.

The blanket chest I designed and made for a family in New Hampshire is a piece of furniture that could have been just another unremarkable dovetailed box, but it is redeemed by frame-and-panel construction that allows for greater play with forms and

materials. It pleases me to think that many years from now, someone will open this chest on a snowy December night, pull out a down comforter as proof against the cold, and think, "What a beautiful chest."

LEGS DOUBLE AS STILES

A chest made of four solid slabs dovetailed together looks too heavy and traditional for my taste, and I can assemble frames and panels much more quickly than I can cut long rows of dovetails. Frame-and-panel construction has more going for it than lightness and economy of labor: It adds depth and shadow lines to the look of a piece, and it allows the use of contrasting wood—something you can't do with mitered or dovetailed chests made only from flat panels.

My client wanted a fresh design that incorporated elements of two of my previous frame-and-panel chests. In a departure from one of the older designs, I decided to eliminate the stiles of the frame-and-panel sides and join the top and bottom rails directly to the legs so that the legs themselves serve as stiles (see the drawing on p. 99). This legs-as-stiles approach, which I had first tried nine years ago on a cabinet, allows for simplified construction and a lighter look than full frame-and-panel sides attached to separate legs. (Squinting at the blanket chest, you can almost imagine away the light-colored panels, leaving behind an open frame of thin, table-like legs and rails.) A gentle curve in the bottom rail helps the legs visually lift the chest off the floor.

The frames are made of cherry and the panels are of curly maple. The legs are made from 8/4 lumber, lightened and made more interesting by chamfering on all four sides. To add even more visual character and a form of decorative detail, I brought the double tenons of the front and rear rails through and let them stand ⅛ in. proud of the legs. And to transform the top from a typical rectangular shape into a more pleasing and interesting form, I decided to curve the ends of the lid, carrying through the motif of the curved bottom rails.

MORTISE-AND-TENON JOINTS HOLD THE PANELS TOGETHER

Mortise-and-tenon joints, in one form or another, are the basis for all good furniture construction, and this blanket chest is no exception. As in a post-and-beam house or a post-and-rail fence, mortise-and-tenon joints draw horizontal and vertical pieces of furniture together simply and rigidly. Used with frame-and-panel construction, these joints make furniture that accommodates seasonal changes in the wood better than any other method.

The architect Louis Kahn said that the joint was the beginning of all ornament, and this holds true for the wedged, double through-tenons on my blanket chest. I worried that through-tenons would detract from the lines of the legs, but now that I've done them, I'd do them again. Details like these through-tenons add mystery because people at first wonder why they're there, and yet they take away mystery because they ultimately reveal the nature of the construction. I've noticed at shows that people make a beeline to just such details.

CAREFUL PREPARATION PAYS DIVIDENDS DURING MORTISING

I always sticker more wood to acclimate in my shop than I think I'll need for a project, and I take a few shavings from each board with a block plane to give me a clearer view of its grain and color. For the legs, I wanted straight grain—nothing wild—so that no one leg would detract from the others. I also wanted consistency in the grain of the rails so that the figured curly maple would stand out. To match the grain on the top and bottom rails of a given side, I chose boards wider than 8 in., wide enough that I could rip them into a 3-in. top rail and a 3½-in. bottom rail. Because my design called for relatively narrow rails, I felt I could use flatsawn cherry instead of more expensive quartersawn cherry. Flatsawn lumber will expand and contract more than quartersawn lumber. But with a narrow rail, the difference will be negligible.

I began by roughing out the four legs. I always cut pieces to length oversized by a few inches. I keep an eye out for end-checking and surface defects and plan my cuts around them. If, when I am laying out the pieces, it looks as though one might have a streak of sapwood showing, then I'll rough out five legs. And I always mill a few test pieces. Using test pieces to set up joinery cuts helps ensure my good pieces will be right on. In making any piece of furniture, my time and labor far outweigh the cost of using a few extra inches of wood here and there. This is not a place to be stingy.

I chose to make all the mortises and tenons ⅜ in. thick, with the tenons on the bottom rail a little wider than those on the top rail. The side rails and the frame for the top are put together with blind, not through-tenons. After I determined their locations, I laid out the mortises and tenons on the legs and rails with a marking gauge and a very sharp pencil.

There are many ways to cut mortises, ranging from using hollow-chisel machines and plunge routers with spiral end mills to chopping them out by hand the old-fashioned way. I use an Italian-made slot-mortising machine to cut mortises in my shop. The machine can use either a Clico slot-mortise miller bit (available from Garrett Wade; 800-221-2942) or a spiral end mill (available from Woodcraft Supply; 800-225-1153). A slot-mortising machine is expensive, but it's extremely accurate once you've set it up, and it's a pleasure to use. I've never understood why the Taiwanese haven't made a less expensive one.

A slot mortiser leaves a mortise with rounded ends. I prefer the look of a squared tenon in an exposed through-mortise joint, so on the blanket chest legs, I squared up the mortises by hand with a bench chisel. Working on the outside face of the leg, I made starter cuts on the sides of the rounded mortise and then cut out the waste at the end. The English would have cut a tapered mortise to accept the flared shape of a wedged tenon. I didn't make a big deal of

it, but I did cut a little heavy on the end line and chiseled a slight taper.

When I cut the mortises, I also used my slot mortiser to cut the grooves that receive the maple panels. Because both the mortises and grooves are centered on the legs, I had only to change the bit. You could also use a router or a dado blade on the tablesaw to cut the grooves.

For cutting tenons, I prefer a tablesaw. I made the shoulder cuts first, using a tenon jig that safely secured the rails perpendicular to the table. As always when cutting tenons, I used a test piece to check the settings of the tablesaw. I removed the waste between the double tenons with a bandsaw, and cut slots for the wedges two-thirds through the tenons with a backsaw.

Once all the mortise-and-tenon joinery was cut, I dry-fit each tenon to its own designated mortise. I strive for an exact fit right off the machine. If I'm going to use machines, I insist on obtaining a high degree of accuracy. I've put a lot of time into adjusting and keeping my saws, jointer and planer tuned up. Those machines and my trifocals ensure the precision I've grown to expect.

A COVE BIT SHAPES THE PANELS

I feel as though we've become anesthetized to frame-and-panel construction because of kitchen cabinetry, much of which has been derivative of traditional furniture. I try not to make furniture that looks like a kitchen cabinet. So I milled the five curly maple panels that make up the sides and the top of the blanket chest from solid stock glued together with butt joints at the seams. I raised the panels by cutting a cove around the perimeter on the outside surface, allowing for a very narrow reveal between the frame pieces and the cove.

For the cove cut, I used a router table with a standard high-speed-steel, ⅜-in. cove bit. To increase the height of the cove, I stood the panels on end, against the fence, and ran them vertically through the router. This way, I could make use of the ¾-in. height of the cove bit rather than its smaller radius.

Because the legs serve as the stiles of the frame-and-panel sides, they are mortised for the rail tenons as well as grooved for the panel tongues. Both the mortises and grooves are centered on the inside faces of the leg, so layout is straightforward.

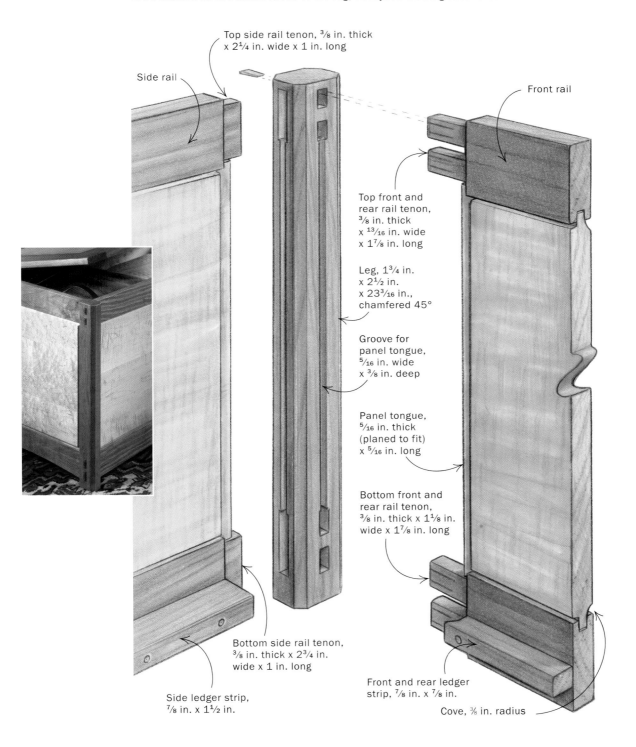

Top side rail tenon, 3/8 in. thick x 2 1/4 in. wide x 1 in. long

Side rail

Front rail

Top front and rear rail tenon, 3/8 in. thick x 13/16 in. wide x 1 7/8 in. long

Leg, 1 3/4 in. x 2 1/2 in. x 23 3/16 in., chamfered 45°

Groove for panel tongue, 5/16 in. wide x 3/8 in. deep

Panel tongue, 5/16 in. thick (planed to fit) x 5/16 in. long

Bottom front and rear rail tenon, 3/8 in. thick x 1 1/8 in. wide x 1 7/8 in. long

Bottom side rail tenon, 3/8 in. thick x 2 3/4 in. wide x 1 in. long

Side ledger strip, 7/8 in. x 1 1/2 in.

Front and rear ledger strip, 7/8 in. x 7/8 in.

Cove, 3/8 in. radius

The frame-and-panel sides of this chest are a departure from the solid sides and dovetailed corners of a traditional chest. Unlike solid box construction, frame-and-panel construction creates interesting shadow lines and allows for the use of contrasting woods.

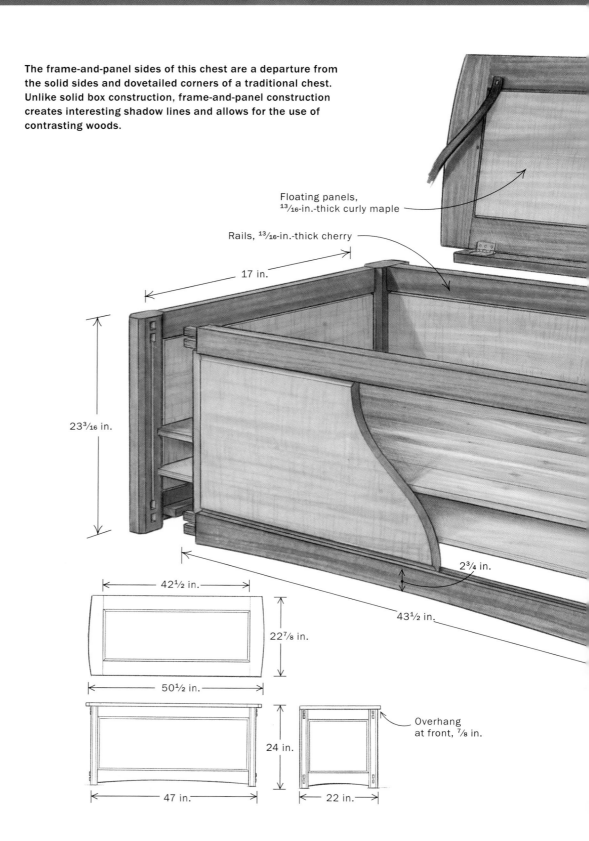

Floating panels, 13/16-in.-thick curly maple

Rails, 13/16-in.-thick cherry

17 in.

23³/₁₆ in.

2³/₄ in.

43¹/₂ in.

42¹/₂ in.

22⁷/₈ in.

50¹/₂ in.

24 in.

47 in.

22 in.

Overhang at front, ⁷/₈ in.

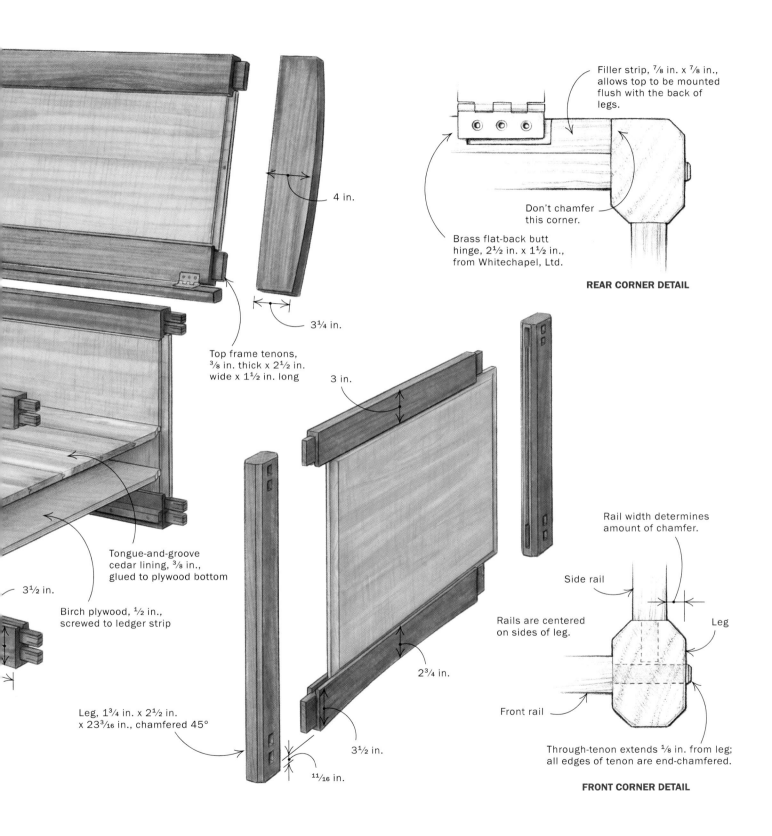

Filler strip, 7/8 in. x 7/8 in., allows top to be mounted flush with the back of legs.

Don't chamfer this corner.

Brass flat-back butt hinge, 2½ in. x 1½ in., from Whitechapel, Ltd.

REAR CORNER DETAIL

4 in.

3¼ in.

Top frame tenons, 3/8 in. thick x 2½ in. wide x 1½ in. long

3 in.

Tongue-and-groove cedar lining, 3/8 in., glued to plywood bottom

3½ in.

Birch plywood, ½ in., screwed to ledger strip

2¾ in.

Leg, 1¾ in. x 2½ in. x 23³/16 in., chamfered 45°

3½ in.

11/16 in.

Rail width determines amount of chamfer.

Side rail

Leg

Rails are centered on sides of leg.

Front rail

Through-tenon extends 1/8 in. from leg; all edges of tenon are end-chamfered.

FRONT CORNER DETAIL

■ One side at a time

To avoid gluing up too much at once, assemble the front and rear panels first.

1. Glue the double through-tenons of the top and bottom rails into a mortised leg.

2. Fit the panel into the grooves in the rails and leg without glue.

3. Glue up the other leg, and wedge the through-tenons.

4. Join the completed front and rear with the side rails and panels to form a carcase.

PIN THE PANELS FROM THE INSIDE

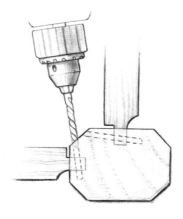

Pin the center of each vertical tongue to the legs with a 1/8-in. dowel, so the panels will expand and contract evenly at the top and bottom rails. Angle the hole for the pin to prevent the drill from damaging the sides of the panels.

I took slight incremental cuts, about 1/16 in. at a pass, to avoid burning the maple. This improves consistency and saves time and frustration. And I ran each panel through consecutively before raising the bit. Experience has taught me to be careful not to bull through this process. Only a newly sharpened bit will do; if the bit is borderline dull, it will burn. And I find that high speed steel is less likely than carbide to burn a workpiece. For most woodworking projects, I think carbide has been over-hyped.

After I finished cutting the coves on all five panels, I used a dado blade in my table-saw to remove enough material to make a tongue that fits into the grooves previously cut in the legs and rails. The grooves were 3/8 in. deep, so I made the tongues 5/16 in. long, allowing 1/16 in. for expansion. In sizing panels, it's important to allow enough room for seasonal expansion and contraction.

Often I have to fine-tune the width of a panel tongue by using a rabbet plane to shave the shoulder.

I pre-finished all the curly maple panels before assembly, because it's easier to get a finish on the cove edges this way. On the inside surfaces, I brushed on three coats of shellac. Shellac will not impart any unpleasant odor to blankets or sweaters stored inside the chest. On the outside of the panels, I used a linseed oil and turpentine mixture, wiping off any excess oil (as it began to tack up) with cotton rags. I took great care to dispose of the rags by putting them in a bucket of water.

ASSEMBLY IS EASY

With all the parts prepared, I assembled the chest in sections (see the photos on the facing page). The front and rear sections each consist of two legs, top and bottom rails and a floating panel. I glued and clamped the front and rear sections separately. (I prefer Titebond Extend glue, which I buy from Woodcraft Supply, because it provides a little more working time for putting together many parts at once.) At this time, I wedged the exposed through-tenons with precut maple wedges, wetted with a dab of glue. I also pinned the vertical centers of the panel tongues to the legs so that the panels will expand and contract evenly in the top and bottom rails (see the drawing on the facing page). When the glue on the front and rear frames had set, I then glued and clamped the whole chest together, joining the front and rear sections with the top and bottom rails of the sides. I was careful not to forget to put in the maple side panels.

After the four sides were together, I attached bottom ledger strips with screws and glue, and screwed a ½-in. birch plywood bottom panel to the ledger. I painted the plywood panel with milk paint (which, like the shellac, won't impart an odor). With a few lengthwise beads, I glued a tongue-and-groove aromatic cedar lining on top of the plywood to make the floor of the chest smell good (see the photos at top right). A little play in the tongue-and-groove joints

LEDGER STRIPS SUPPORT A PLYWOOD BOTTOM PANEL painted with odorless milk paint (above). A liner of tongue-and-groove aromatic cedar (left) is glued on top of the plywood and is notched to fit around the legs.

A FILLER STRIP HOLDS THE HINGES. The strip is glued to the rear top rail and butts against the rear legs, whose inside back corners remain unchamfered.

and glue on only a few boards allow the cedar lining to expand and contract without busting up the chest. I also glued up the frame-and-panel top, which is essentially a door mounted on brass butt hinges.

Once the top was glued up, I laid out the curves on the ends, using spline weights and a plastic spline. I cut the curves with a sabersaw and then cleaned up the edges with a block plane and sandpaper. Before setting the hinges, I glued a filler strip to the rear top rail, between the two rear legs (see the photos above). To keep the lid from swinging too far back, I installed a leather strap. The leather adds a warm touch to the chest without sacrificing strength.

IAN INGERSOLL

Craftsman Wall Cabinet

There is always a spot for a wall cabinet, especially a small one. This Craftsman-style piece is modeled after a clock, and at a little more than a foot wide it fits well in almost any tight, vertical space. I made it out of butternut, an underused, medium-toned wood that works easily. Because this cabinet was destined for a kitchen, I outfitted the inside to accommodate spices, but the same-sized cabinet could hold anything from pottery to small books. The shelves, in this case, are spaced to fit off-the-rack spice bottles, with the bottom shelf roomy enough for larger, bulk-sized decanters. The tilting drawer at the bottom is made to fit large packages of tea.

When it comes to construction, the simplest answers are often best. On this small, vertical cabinet, I could have dovetailed the case, but I saw no need to spend the time when countersunk and plugged screws

would do. And on such a simple piece, I didn't want anything to detract attention from the door, where I spent most of the design and construction energy. I used a flat panel at the bottom of the door to cover the drawer and bulk items, but at the top I installed glass to show off the nicer-looking spice bottles and to make the piece a bit more interesting. Over the single piece of glass, I installed muntins, giving the appearance of two-over-two panes of glass.

Begin by milling up the lumber: The top and bottom are 1 in. thick; the sides, door rails and stiles are ¾ in. thick; the drawer parts are ⅝ in. thick; the back and shelves are ½ in. thick; the muntins and door panel are ¼ in. thick.

BUILDING THE BASIC CASE

Don't waste energy with overly complex methods of building the case. Use ¾-in.- and ½-in.-thick stock and trim everything to width and length on the tablesaw. Set up the tablesaw to cut ½-in. dadoes for the shelves. Use a stop on your miter gauge to ensure that the dadoes in the back and sides will line up. It's not really necessary to dado the back panel for the shelves, but doing so eases glue-up.

The first step in the process is rabbeting the top and bottom—because the same stop location can be used for each—on all three pieces. Then locate each shelf and set the stop on your miter gauge. When the dadoes have been cut on each of the three pieces, they should all line up perfectly. On the two sides, use the same setup to cut another ½-in. dado, inset ½ in. and ¼ in. deep, to house the back panel.

With the dadoes lined up on the back and sides of the case, trim all of the shelves to width and length and install the ⅜-in. drawer stop on the bottom shelf. Locate the position by marking off the width of the drawer front, then inset the stop another 3/16 in. A screw holds the stop in place and allows it to pivot. On the bottom shelf, cut a ¼-in. by ¼-in. groove with the dado setup on the tablesaw. This groove will work as a hinging mechanism for the tilting drawer. With the drawer stop installed and the groove cut, you can glue up the case, which should go smoothly on such a small piece.

INSTALLING THE TOP AND BOTTOM

Making the bottom of this case out of 1-in.-thick stock gives the piece a grounded look. Just remember to leave a ½-in. overhang on the front and sides, and make sure you account for the door. Rout a 1-in. bullnose on the edges of the bottom and leave the decoration for the top.

The treatment for the top is one I regularly use on tabletops. It lends the piece a nice, finished look and helps draw your attention to the glass panels in the door. Start by cutting a ¼-in. bead on the outside edge at the front and sides. Then establish the overhang, in this case 1½ in., and mark a line there. If it feels safe, use the tablesaw. With the piece held upright, sight down the raised blade and adjust the angle until it enters at the bottom of the bead and exits at the overhang line. You can achieve the same results by cutting to the line with a handplane. The result is a rounded top edge that angles back sharply toward the case. Both the top and bottom are simply screwed onto the case and pegged.

BUILDING THE DRAWER

When you open this case, the drawer at the bottom is a nice surprise. Instead of sliding as a normal drawer would, this tall drawer

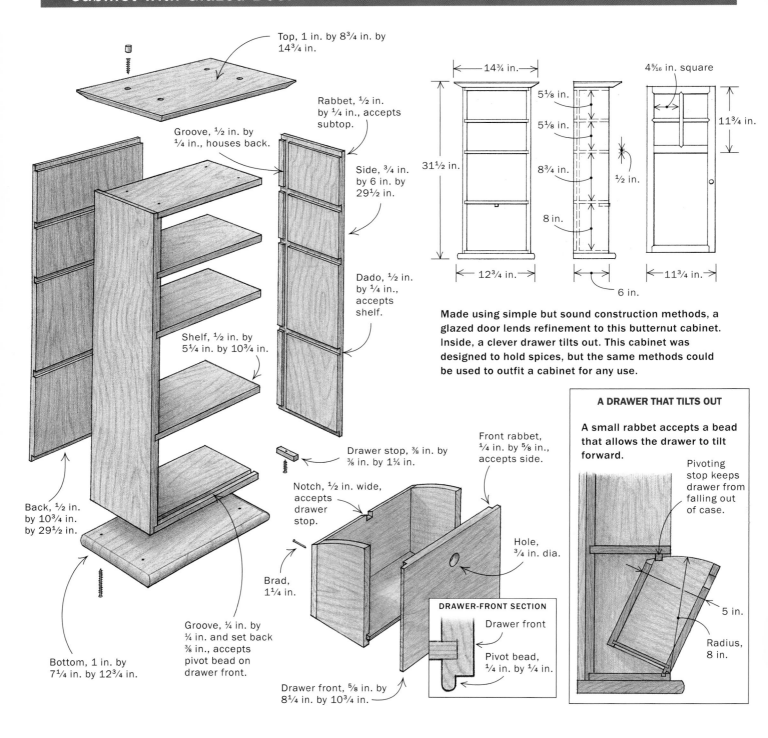

Top, 1 in. by 8¾ in. by 14¾ in.

Groove, ½ in. by ¼ in., houses back.

Rabbet, ½ in. by ¼ in., accepts subtop.

Side, ¾ in. by 6 in. by 29½ in.

Dado, ½ in. by ¼ in., accepts shelf.

Shelf, ½ in. by 5¼ in. by 10¾ in.

Back, ½ in. by 10¾ in. by 29½ in.

Bottom, 1 in. by 7¼ in. by 12¾ in.

Groove, ¼ in. by ¼ in. and set back ⅜ in., accepts pivot bead on drawer front.

Drawer stop, ⅜ in. by ⅜ in. by 1¼ in.

Notch, ½ in. wide, accepts drawer stop.

Brad, 1¼ in.

Drawer front, ⅝ in. by 8¼ in. by 10¾ in.

Front rabbet, ¼ in. by ⅝ in., accepts side.

Hole, ¾ in. dia.

14¾ in.

5⅛ in.

5⅛ in.

8¾ in.

8 in.

31½ in.

12¾ in.

½ in.

6 in.

4⁵⁄₁₆ in. square

11¾ in.

11¾ in.

Made using simple but sound construction methods, a glazed door lends refinement to this butternut cabinet. Inside, a clever drawer tilts out. This cabinet was designed to hold spices, but the same methods could be used to outfit a cabinet for any use.

DRAWER-FRONT SECTION

Drawer front

Pivot bead, ¼ in. by ¼ in.

A DRAWER THAT TILTS OUT

A small rabbet accepts a bead that allows the drawer to tilt forward.

Pivoting stop keeps drawer from falling out of case.

5 in.

Radius, 8 in.

tilts forward and down so that you can reach in for tea or whatever you decide to store inside. The sides and back are rounded so that the drawer slides open easily with the pull—nothing more than a ¾-in.-dia. hole in the front—but the stop keeps the drawer from falling out on the floor. By twisting

the stop you can easily remove the whole drawer for easy cleaning or restocking.

The four sides of the drawer are cut to size and dadoed with a ¼-in. blade to accept the plywood bottom. Make sure you cut the front ¼ in. wider so that there will be enough material to form the pivoting bead

Making an easy bridle joint

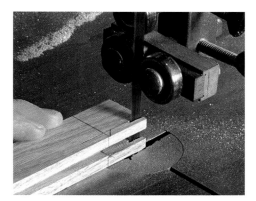

AN EASY BUT REFINED DOOR DETAIL. With the rail grooved and the mortise cut, a bandsaw trims away the inside edge to accept the stile.

A MITERED DOOR JOINT. With a 45° miter jig clamped to the rail, a chisel pares to the line. This simple detail lends a framed and finished look to the door.

A PERFECT FIT. It's best to work out any problems before you begin glue-up. A dry run ensures that everything fits and that the bridle joints pull tight.

along the bottom. The side edges of the front and back are rabbeted to accept the sides. The two sides and the back are all shaped on the bandsaw, and a small notch is removed from the top center of the back to allow for the drawer stop.

To provide the tilting action, the bottom of the front of the drawer has a ¼-in. bead that protrudes down into the groove cut into the bottom of the case. Rout this bead on the inside of the drawer front, then use a dado blade to remove the front edge. This bead should fit nicely into the groove on the bottom of the case and allow the drawer to fall forward. The drawer is glued up with the bottom floating in the dadoes, and a few brads in the sides and back hold everything in place.

BUILDING AND GLAZING THE DOOR

The bulk of the work on this small piece involves the cabinet's natural focal point: the door. First, cut the rails and stiles to 1¼ in. wide and trim them to length. Use bridle joints to frame the door. Bridle joints not only offer plenty of strength, but they also make easy work of measuring. Because the tenons run the full width of the door, simply mark the length of each piece off the case itself. The center rail is the one excep-

An Easy and Elegant Door

To lend a more elegant look to a simple door, muntins overlay a single piece of glass, giving the appearance that there are four separate panes.

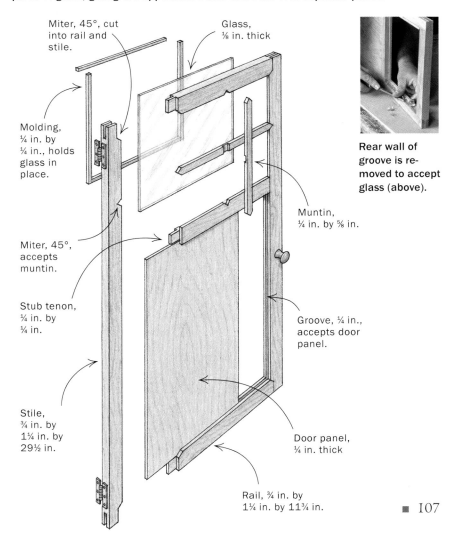

Miter, 45°, cut into rail and stile.

Glass, ⅛ in. thick

Molding, ¼ in. by ¼ in., holds glass in place.

Miter, 45°, accepts muntin.

Stub tenon, ¼ in. by ¼ in.

Stile, ¾ in. by 1¼ in. by 29½ in.

Muntin, ¼ in. by ⅝ in.

Groove, ¼ in., accepts door panel.

Door panel, ¼ in. thick

Rail, ¾ in. by 1¼ in. by 11¾ in.

Rear wall of groove is removed to accept glass (above).

Setting muntins in place

PANES FOR THE GLASS. With two 45° cuts on each muntin end, the muntins are laid in place, and the miters are marked on the rails and stiles.

CUTTING MITERS IN THE RAILS AND STILES. To accept the muntin ends, a small gentleman's saw cuts miters on the door frame.

CROSSING THE GLASS. To give the appearance of divided panes of glass, muntins are added. The half-lap joint is cut on the tablesaw (below).

rail and stile grooves full length on the tablesaw.

Use a ¼-in. dado setup to cut the grooves on the inside faces of the rails and stiles. For the median and upper rails, you also remove the inside portion of the groove so that the glass can slide into place after the door has been assembled.

Using the same dado setup and a simple jig that fits over the tablesaw to hold the stiles upright, raise the blade to 1 in. and cut a tenon slot on the ends of the rails. Adjust the fence so that in two passes you're able to leave the ¼-in.-thick tenon. At the bandsaw, trim down the width on the inside of the tenon by ¼ in. You'll notice that this leaves the tenon length ¼ in. shy of mating correctly. A simple miter jig clamped onto the rails and stiles helps guide the chisel for the 45° cuts.

Once you've milled and trimmed a center panel for the bottom of the door, the door can be glued up. When the glue dries, you'll still have to remove the inside of the groove on the upper portion of the door where the glass will be installed. Do this with a straightedge and a box knife, then clean it up with a chisel.

The final touch to this door is to install the muntins. Cut them ⅜ in. wide and center them on the square upper portion of the door. Then use a small gentleman's saw to cut the 45° miters that accommodate the muntins. Once the two pieces press-fit into place, lay one across the other and mark the centers. Cut a ⅛-in. groove where the two cross each other. When installed, a few drops of glue at the groove and on the mitered ends, along with a little tension from the door itself, hold everything in place.

Once the glass slides in, small pieces of molding are used to secure it. All that's left to do is to hang the door and apply the finish and hardware. I used an oil varnish from Waterlox to give this piece a natural look and to provide protection. The hinges I used are antiqued, solid brass H-hinges from Horton Brass (860-635-4400), and the knob is a Shaker-style bronze knob from Colonial Bronze (860-489-9233). After you're done, open the cabinet, reach in the drawer, and fix yourself a cup of tea.

tion, and it is cut with small tenons that fit into ¼-in. by ¼-in. grooves on the stiles.

By cutting the tenons and mortises 1 in. deep instead of 1¼ in. deep (the full width of the rails and stiles), you leave material to cut the 45° haunches at the joints. These haunched tenons not only look more refined, but they also allow you to rip the

STEPHEN LAMONT

Making an End Table

About 10 years ago, I began to tire of my job as a corporate pilot. The work was challenging and enjoyable, but the time away from home put a strain on my family. The job was becoming more technical, too. Temperamentally, I've always been more of a craftsman than a technician.

After considerable soul-searching, I decided to become a furnituremaker. I wanted a solid foundation of basic skills, so I went to England where I trained with Chris Faulkner. He emphasized developing hand-tool skills and building simple, comfortable furniture that asked to be used—a basic tenet of the British Arts-and-Crafts movement. My preferences to this day are for this kind of furniture and for the use of hand tools whenever their use will make a difference.

About two years ago, I designed and built the end table shown in the photo at right. Although it's an original design, many details come from other pieces of furniture in the British Arts-and-Crafts tradition. The joinery is mortise-and-tenon and dovetail throughout.

The construction of the table can be divided into five main steps: stock preparation and panel glue-up; making the front and rear leg assemblies; connecting these two assemblies (including making the shelf and its frame); making and fitting the drawer; and making and attaching the top.

STOCK SELECTION AND PREPARATION

I milled all the stock for this table to within $\frac{1}{16}$ in. of final thickness and width. I also glued up the tabletop, the shelf and the drawer bottom right away to give them time to move a bit before planing them to final thickness. This helps ensure they'll stay flat

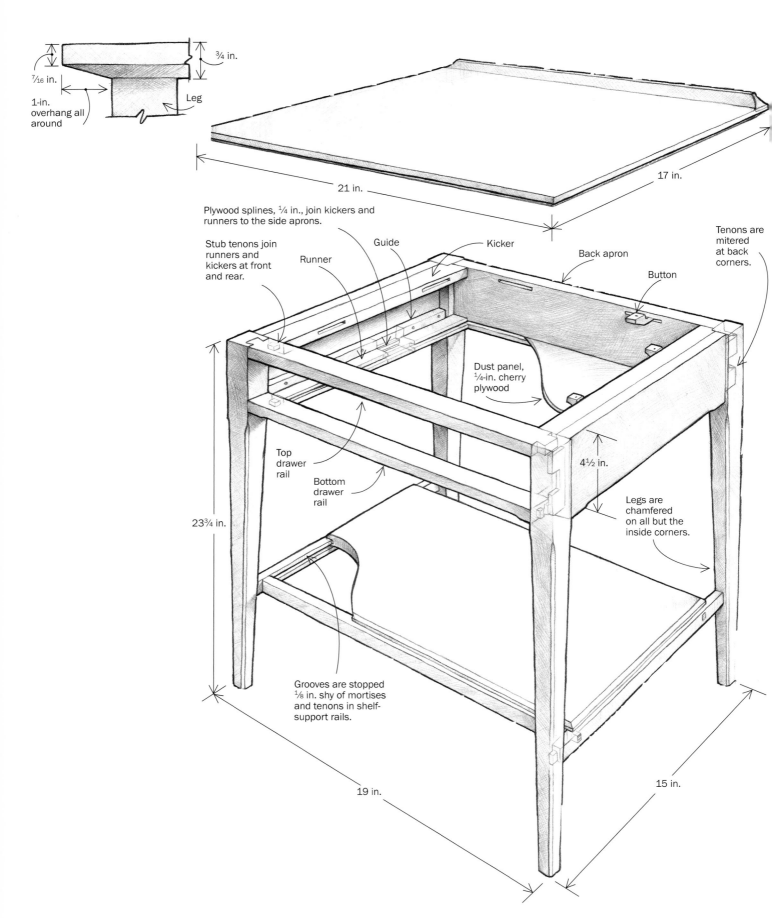

¾ in.

7/16 in.

1-in. overhang all around

Leg

21 in.

17 in.

Plywood splines, ¼ in., join kickers and runners to the side aprons.

Stub tenons join runners and kickers at front and rear.

Runner

Guide

Kicker

Back apron

Button

Tenons are mitered at back corners.

Top drawer rail

Bottom drawer rail

Dust panel, ¼-in. cherry plywood

4½ in.

Legs are chamfered on all but the inside corners.

23¾ in.

Grooves are stopped ⅛ in. shy of mortises and tenons in shelf-support rails.

19 in.

15 in.

in the finished piece. With these three panels in clamps, I dimensioned the rest of the parts to a hair over final thickness. I finish-planed them by hand just before marking out any joinery.

MAKING THE FRONT AND REAR ASSEMBLIES

Layout began with the legs. I numbered them clockwise around the perimeter, beginning with the left front as I faced the piece, writing the numbers on the tops of the legs (see the top left photo on p. 112). This system tells me where each leg goes, which end of a leg is up and which face is which.

Dovetailing the top rail into the front legs

The dovetails that connect the top rail to the front legs taper slightly top to bottom. I used the narrower bottom of the dovetail to lay out the sockets in the legs. The slight taper ensures a snug fit (see the top right photo on p. 112). Don't make the dovetails too large, or you'll weaken the legs.

After I marked, cut and chopped out the sockets, I tested the fit of these dovetails. By using clamping pads and hand screws across the joint, I eliminated the possibility of splitting the leg (see the bottom photo on p. 112). The dovetail should fit snugly but not tightly. Pare the socket, if necessary, until you have a good fit.

Tapering and mortising the legs

I tapered the two inside faces of each leg, beginning 4½ in. down from the top. I removed most of the waste on the jointer and finished the job with a handplane. The tapers must be flat. To avoid planing over a penciled reference line at the top of the taper, I drew hash marks across it. With each stroke of the plane, the lines got shorter. That let me know how close I was getting.

I cut the mortises for this table on a hollow-chisel mortiser. It's quick, and it keeps all the mortises consistent. I made sure all mortises that could be cut with one setting were done at the same time, even if I didn't need the components right away.

Tenoning the aprons and drawer rail

I tenoned the sides, back and lower drawer rail on the tablesaw, using a double-blade tenoning setup. It takes a little time to get the cut right, but once a test piece fits, tenoning takes just a few minutes. After I cut the tenon cheeks on the tablesaw, I bandsawed just shy of the tenon shoulders and then pared to the line.

One wide apron tenon would have meant a very long mortise, weakening the leg. Instead, I divided the wide tenon into two small tenons separated by a stub tenon (see the drawing detail at right). That left plenty of glue-surface area without a big hole in the leg.

Mortising for runners, kickers and buttons

The drawer rides on runners that are mortised into the lower front rail and the back apron. Similarly, the kickers at the tops of the side aprons, which prevent the drawer from drooping when open, are mortised into the top front rail and the back apron. I cut the ¼-in.-wide mortises for the runner and kicker tenons on the back edge of both drawer rails and on the back apron. There are eight mortises for the drawer runners and kickers. Another seven mortises of the same size are for the buttons that attach the top to the table's base—three on the back apron and two on each kicker.

I also cut grooves for the dust panel at this time. The ¼-in.-thick panel is set into the frame of the table just below the drawer. It's a nice touch, even if it's not needed structurally. I cut the grooves for the panel into the bottom of the back apron and into the back of the drawer rail. (I cut the dust-panel grooves in the drawer runners later.) Then I made a test-fit with a scrap of the same ¼-in. cherry plywood used for the panel.

Chamfering and gluing up

Stopped chamfers are routed on the legs and aprons of this table, each terminating in a carved lamb's tongue. I stopped routing just shy of the area to be carved and then carved the tongue and the little shoulder in three steps, as shown in the photos on p. 113.

■ Joinery Details

Careful joinery adds to the strength of this Arts-and-Crafts table without compromising its delicate lines.

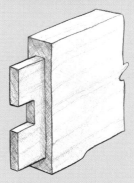

APRON TO LEG
Two small tenons connected by a stub tenon provide nearly the same glue-surface area and resistance to twisting as a full-width tenon, without weakening the leg as much.

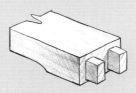

LOWER DRAWER RAIL TO LEG
Two small, parallel tenons effectively double the glue-surface area that would be available on a single tenon on this delicate frame member.

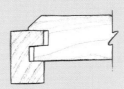

SHELF-TO-SHELF SUPPORT RAIL
The bottom tongue of the shelf's edge nests in the groove of the rail, providing a positive yet inconspicuous connection. The shelf can expand and contract freely with changes in humidity.

KEEPING TRACK OF THE LEGS is easier when they're numbered on top, clockwise from the front left. This system helps prevent layout errors.

MARKING OUT THE DOVETAIL SOCKET. Scribing the socket from the bottom of the slightly tapered dovetail ensures a good fit in the leg.

CHECKING THE FIT OF THE TOP-RAIL DOVETAIL. A hand screw prevents a leg from splitting if the dovetail is too big. The fit should be snug but not tight.

Gluing up the table base is a two-step process. First I connected the front legs with the top and bottom drawer rails and the back legs with the back apron. To prevent the legs from toeing in or out because of clamping pressure, I inserted spacers between the legs at their feet and clamped both the top and bottom. Then I check for square, measuring diagonally from corner to corner (see the photo on p. 114). It ensures that the assembly is square and that the legs are properly spaced.

CONNECTING THE FRONT AND REAR ASSEMBLIES

To hold the legs in position while I measured for the drawer runners and kickers and, later, to get the spacing on shelf-support rails correct, I made a simple frame of hardboard and wooden corner blocks (see the top photo on p. 115). The frame ensures the assembly is square and the legs are properly spaced. After I marked the shoulder-to-shoulder lengths for the runners and kickers, I cut and fit the stub tenons that join these pieces to the front and rear assemblies. The back ends of the runners and kickers must be notched to fit around the inside corners of the legs.

Runners, kickers and dust panel I cut the ¼-in. grooves for the dust panel in the drawer runners next. I also cut grooves for the splines with which I connected the drawer runners and kickers to the sides of the table. There are 10 grooves in all—one each on the inside and outside edges of the drawer runners, one on the outside edge of each of the kickers and two in each side for the splines.

Then I dry-clamped the table and made sure the tops of the kickers were flush with the top edges of the sides, the tops of the runners flush with the top of the drawer rail and the bottoms of the runners flush with the bottom edges of the sides. Then I cut the dust panel to size, test-fit it and set it aside until glue-up.

Building the shelf frame and shelf The shelf on this table is a floating panel captured by a frame made of four rails. The two rails that run front to back are tenoned into the legs; the other two are joined to the first pair with through-wedged tenons.

I put the dry-assembled table into the hardboard frame and clamped the legs to the blocks. Then I clamped the pair of rails that will be tenoned into the legs against the inside surfaces of the legs and marked the shoulder of each tenon (see the bottom photo on p. 115). I also marked the rails for orientation so that the shoulders can be mated correctly with the legs.

Tenons were cut and fit next. With the rails dry-clamped into the legs, I measured for the two remaining rails to be joined to the first pair. I laid out and cut the through-mortises in the first set of rails, chopping halfway in from each side to prevent tearout. I cut the tenons on the second set of rails, assembled the frame and marked the through-tenons with a pencil line for wedge orientation. So they don't split the rails, the wedges must be perpendicular to the grain of the mortised rail.

I flared the sides of the through-mortises (not the tops and bottoms) so the outside of the mortise is about $\frac{1}{16}$ in. wider than the inside. This taper, which goes about three-quarters of the way into the mortise, lets the wedges splay the tenon, locking the rail into the mortise like a dovetail.

Next I marked the location of the wedge kerfs in each tenon, scribing a line from both sides of the tenon with a marking gauge for uniformity. I cut the kerfs at a slight angle. Wedges must fill both the kerf and the gap in the widened mortise, so they need to be just over $\frac{1}{16}$ in. thick at their widest.

An interlocking tongue and groove connects the shelf to the rails that support it (see the drawing detail on p. 111). Using a $\frac{1}{4}$-in. slot cutter in my table-mounted router, I cut the groove in the rails, working out the fit on

■ Carving a lamb's tongue

1. Pare to marked baseline. Strive for a fair, even curve, and cut down toward the chamfer.

2. Tap a stop for the shoulder at the baseline. Avoid cutting too deeply; just a light tap is needed.

3. Pare into stop to create a shoulder. You have to cut toward the shoulder, so take light cuts and watch which way the grain is running. If you must pare against the grain, make sure your chisel is freshly honed. ■

test pieces first. The slots are $\frac{1}{4}$ in. deep. I stopped the grooves in the rails $\frac{1}{8}$ in. or so short of the mortises on the side rails and short of the tenon shoulders on the front and back rails. I notched the shelf to fit at the corners (see the drawing on p. 110).

I measured the space between the rails of the shelf frame and added $\frac{1}{2}$ in. in each direction to get the shelf dimensions. I cut the tongue on all four edges on the router table.

CHECK DIAGONALS TO MAKE SURE ASSEMBLIES ARE GLUED UP SQUARE. Clamps and a spacer at the bottom of the legs prevent the clamping pressure at the top from causing the legs to toe in or out.

Gluing up the shelf-frame assembly

Before gluing up the shelf frame, I routed hollows in clamp pads to fit over the through-tenons on two of the shelf rails. Then I began gluing up the shelf assembly. I applied glue sparingly in the mortises and on the tenons so I wouldn't accidentally glue the shelf in place. I pulled the joints tight with clamps and then removed the clamps temporarily so I could insert the wedges.

After tapping the lightly glue-coated wedges into the kerfs in the tenons, I reclamped the frame. I checked diagonals and adjusted the clamps until the assembly was square. Once the glue was dry, I sawed off the protruding tenons and wedges and planed them flush.

Overall glue-up With the shelf frame glued up, the entire table was ready to be assembled. I began the large front-to-back glue-up by dry-clamping the front and back leg assemblies, sides, runners, kickers (with splines), dust panel and shelf assembly. I made adjustments and then glued up.

I made and fit the drawer guides next (see the drawing for placement). I glued the

guides to both the sides and the runners and screwed them to the sides with deeply countersunk brass screws.

I did a thorough cleanup of the table in preparation for drawer fitting. I removed remaining glue, ironed out dents and sanded the entire piece with 120-grit sandpaper on a block. I gently pared sharp corners, taking care not to lose overall crispness.

THE DRAWER

I particularly enjoy making and fitting drawers. A well-made drawer that whispers in and out gives me great satisfaction. I use the traditional British system of drawer-making, which produces what my teachers called a piston fit. The process is painstaking, but the results are well-worth the effort. That, however, is a story for another day.

MAKING AND ATTACHING THE TOP

After I thicknessed and cut the top to size, I placed it face down on my bench. I set the glued-up base upside down on the top and oriented it so it would have a 1-in. overhang all around. I marked the positions of the outside corners and connected them with a pencil line around the perimeter. This line is one edge of the bevel on the underside of the top. Then I used a marking gauge to strike a line 7/16 in. from the top surface on all four edges. Connecting the two lines at the edges created the bevel angle (see the drawing on p. 110). I roughed out the bevel on the tablesaw and cleaned it up with a plane. The bevels should appear to grow out of the tops of the legs.

Making and attaching the coved lip

The cove at the back of the top is a strip set into a rabbet at the back. I cut the cove from the same board I used for the top so that grain and color would match closely. I ripped the cove strip on the tablesaw and handplaned it to fit the rabbet. I shaped the strip on the router table, leaving the point at which it intersects the top slightly proud. To provide even clamping pressure, I used a

SIMPLE FRAME KEEPS LEGS SPACED ACCURATELY and the base of the table square. A ¼-in.-thick piece of hardboard and some scrap blocks make up this handy frame. With the legs properly spaced, the author can mark the shoulders of the shelf-frame rail against the tapered legs as well as take precise measurements for runner and kicker lengths.

rabbeted caul, clamping both down and in (see the photo at right).

When the glue was dry, I planed the back and the ends of the cove flush with the top. To form a smooth transition between top and cove in front, I used a curved scraper, followed by sandpaper on a block shaped to fit the cove. I frequently checked the transition with my hand and sanded a wider swath toward the end. It's easy to go too far and have a nasty dip in front of the cove.

I drew the ends of the cove with a French curve and then shaped the ends with a coping saw, chisel and sandpaper. The curve should blend into the tabletop seamlessly.

Finishing up with oil After finish-sanding, I applied several coats of raw linseed oil

diluted with mineral spirits in a 50/50 mix, a few more coats of straight linseed oil and, finally, two to three coats of tung oil to harden the surface. I let the oil dry thoroughly between coats. After the last coat of oil was dry, I rubbed the surface down with a Scotch-Brite pad and gave the table a few coats of paste wax. The drawer was the exception: Aside from the face of the drawer front, all other surfaces were finished with wax alone.

Attaching the top I screwed the top to the top-drawer rail from beneath to fix its position at the front. That way, the mating of the bevel with the front rail will be correct and any seasonal movement of the top will be at the back. I attached the top to the base with buttons on the sides and in the rear.

RABBETED CLAMPING BLOCK HELPS PROVIDE PRESSURE IN TWO PLANES. The author clamps down the cove strip with six C-clamps and into the rabbet with six bar clamps. A spring clamp on each end closes any visible gaps at the ends.

MARIO RODRIGUEZ

Pear Mantel Clock

My daughter Isabel's seventh birthday was fast approaching, and I wanted to build her something special. She had recently learned to tell time, so a clock seemed like the perfect way to mark the occasion. I designed the clock in the Arts-and-Crafts style; it looks somewhat contemporary but still has a traditional feel (see the photo at left). The joinery is simple, just stub tenons and dadoes, most of which can be cut quickly on a router table and tablesaw.

The clock consists of eight parts: the top, bottom and two sides, the middle shelf assembly, veneered panels for the face and back of the clock, and a door below the middle shelf. The clock is just a bit taller than 16 in. As a result, not a lot of wood is required to build it, and the planing, sanding and finishing don't take very long.

This clock is made of pear, which has a very mild grain that lets the clock's design dominate. A coarsely grained or heavily figured wood could overpower a clock of this size.

USE ROUTER TABLE AND TABLESAW FOR JOINERY

The two sides of the clock are dadoed into the top, and the lower and middle shelves are dadoed to the sides. I routed these stopped dadoes as well as the grooves for the back panel and face panel on the router table. The dadoes are all ¼ in. deep by ¼ in. wide. I moved the router-table fence over a hair for the grooves, which are just slightly

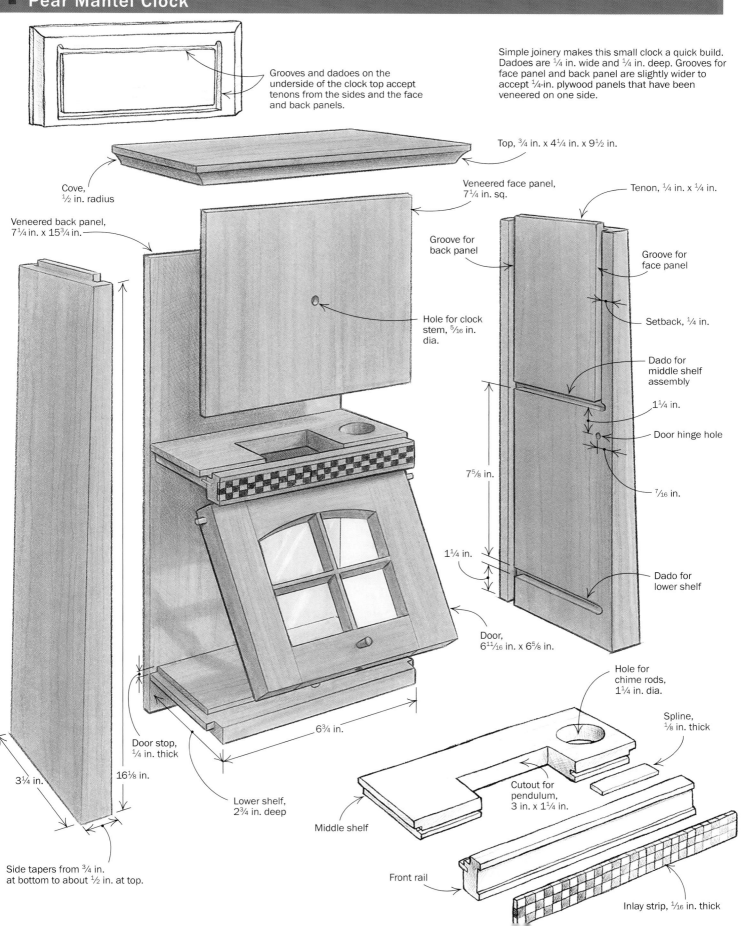

Grooves and dadoes on the underside of the clock top accept tenons from the sides and the face and back panels.

Simple joinery makes this small clock a quick build. Dadoes are ¼ in. wide and ¼ in. deep. Grooves for face panel and back panel are slightly wider to accept ¼-in. plywood panels that have been veneered on one side.

Top, ¾ in. x 4¼ in. x 9½ in.

Cove, ½ in. radius

Veneered face panel, 7¼ in. sq.

Tenon, ¼ in. x ¼ in.

Veneered back panel, 7¼ in. x 15¾ in.

Groove for back panel

Groove for face panel

Hole for clock stem, 5/16 in. dia.

Setback, ¼ in.

Dado for middle shelf assembly

1¼ in.

Door hinge hole

7⁵⁄₈ in.

7/16 in.

1¼ in.

Dado for lower shelf

Door, 6¹¹⁄₁₆ in. x 6⁵⁄₈ in.

Hole for chime rods, 1¼ in. dia.

Spline, ⅛ in. thick

Door stop, ¼ in. thick

Cutout for pendulum, 3 in. x 1¼ in.

6¾ in.

16⅛ in.

3¼ in.

Lower shelf, 2¾ in. deep

Middle shelf

Side tapers from ¾ in. at bottom to about ½ in. at top.

Front rail

Inlay strip, 1/16 in. thick

wider to accommodate the face and back panels. I made these from ¼-in. birch plywood, veneering one side with quartersawn pear veneer. To ensure accurate, square cuts on the router table, I used a right-angle jig and cut no more than ⅛ in. deep per pass. With the tablesaw, I cut the corresponding

stub tenons at the top of the case sides and on the ends of the lower and middle shelves. They were cut just a little wide and then fitted by hand.

I tapered the outside faces of the clock sides using a jack plane, taking the sides from ¾ in. at the bottom to just under ½ in. at the

MAKING THE CHECKERED INLAY

The checkerboard band across the middle of the clock is an eye-catching detail, and it really makes the clock. You'll find that it invites close inspection. For best results, use clean, straight material, and don't use any sapwood or wood with other defects. You'd only have to discard several strips of inlay later.

1. Prepare two "sandwiches" of material—one with a lighter wood in between two dark pieces, and the other just the opposite. Width and length aren't critical, but each layer of the laminations must be exactly ¼ in. thick.

2. Plane the edges of each lamination square to the faces, and make sure the edges are free of glue. Crosscut laminations into segments exactly ¼ in. wide.

3. Arrange segments from alternating sandwiches. Glue and clamp them together. Apply pressure down, as well, onto a steel plate or something similar, to ensure even registration all the way across.

4. When the glue has cured, clean up and square the completed checkerboard blank. Bandsaw into 1⁄16-in.-thick strips. Using a knife to pull the thin strips along on the outfeed side of the blade helps. Select the best pieces for the clock inlay. ■

top. This gives the clock a lighter feel and is a detail found on many Arts-and-Crafts clocks made earlier this century. A ½-in. cove routed around the underside of the clock's top gives it a visual lift.

With the top, bottom and sides made and fitted, I planed and scraped the pieces. They were sprayed inside and out with two very thin coats of aerosol nitrocellulose sanding sealer followed by one coat of semigloss lacquer. To keep the joints free of lacquer, I taped the stub tenons and temporarily fit ¼-in. strips into all the dadoes. I scuff-sanded with 320-grit sandpaper between coats. Spraying before assembly allowed easy access into corners, eliminated drips and reduced overspray.

Middle shelf The middle shelf requires a 1¼-in.-dia. hole for chime rods and a 3-in. by 1¼-in. cutout for the pendulum. I made the hole on the drill press with a Forstner bit and cut out the cavity for the pendulum on the tablesaw and bandsaw.

A band of checkerboard inlay is let into a front rail, which is splined to the middle shelf. I used the tablesaw to cut the slot for the ⅛-in. spline and to cut the rabbet in the top of the front rail for the veneered face panel. To create the recess for the checkerboard inlay, I plowed a 1/16-in.-deep groove across the center of the front rail on the tablesaw and planed it smooth and flat. Then I glued and clamped down the checkerboard inlay, which I made of ebony and pear (see the photos on the facing page for a complete description of making the inlay). After the glue had cured, I planed the front rail flush with the inlay (see the top left photo on p. 120), cut the front rail to length and clamped up the middle shelf assembly (see the bottom photo on p. 120). I taped the stub tenons and sprayed the assembly before moving on to the plywood panels for the clock face and back.

VENEER THE FACE AND BACK PANEL

Because I didn't want to worry about wood movement across the width of the clock, I used ¼-in.-thick birch plywood for the face and the back panels.

I veneered the plywood with clear, quartersawn pear. This way, the grain all but disappears. After shooting and taping the veneer seams, I glued the veneer to the plywood using yellow glue and a warm iron. Ordinarily, both sides of the substrate should be veneered so the piece won't cup later. But because both panels are captured, I didn't think it was necessary to veneer their inside faces.

After the glue had dried, I scraped the veneer tape off and cut the panels to size. To mark the center of the face for the clock movement, I struck diagonals from corner to corner and used an awl to make an impression where the lines crossed. Then I scraped and sanded the pear veneer. I finished the face with sanding sealer and semigloss lacquer. By finishing the face before drilling for the clock stem, I didn't have to avoid the hole when I sanded or rubbed with steel wool.

I bored the hole for the clock movement on my drill press and screwed it to the back of the face panel (for part numbers, price and other information on the movement, see the sources box on p. 123). I set the back panel aside until the whole clock was glued up.

GLAZED DOOR SWINGS UP ON DOWEL HINGES

The little door that swings up to provide access to the pendulum is of standard mortise-and-tenon construction. Both top and bottom rails are 1½ in. wide, slightly wider than the stiles. The top rail takes a mild curve, and the bottom accepts a small knob and visually anchors the design. I roughed out the curve in the top rail on the bandsaw, and then I cleaned it up using a template and the template guide on my router table (see the top left photo on p. 122).

After the door frame was glued up, I routed a ¼-in. rabbet all around the inside to accept a pane of glass. I squared the corners of the rabbet and chopped small open-sided mortises in the back side of the door

KERF FRONT RAIL AND MIDDLE SHELF FOR A SPLINE. One pass with each piece over a standard-width blade is plenty. Then just plane the spline to fit.

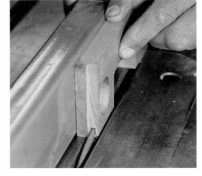

CHECK THE ALIGNMENT (left). The top of the middle shelf and the top of the front rail should be flush. The ¼-in. groove accepts the bottom edge of the face panel.

PLANE THE FRONT RAIL FLUSH. Using a sharp block plane is a quick way to bring the top and bottom edges of the front rail down to the level of the inlay.

MIDDLE SHELF ASSEMBLY

The middle shelf assembly is 2¾ in. deep overall.

Front rail, ½ in. x 1⅛ in.

Groove for face panel, ¼ in. x ¼ in.

Tenon, ¼ in. x ¼ in.

Spline, ⅛ in. x ½ in.

Middle shelf

⟵ 2¾ in. ⟶

Inlay strip, 1⁄16 in. x ¾ in.

MIDDLE SHELF AND FRONT RAIL ARE JOINED WITH A SPLINE. Hand screws provide plenty of clamping pressure, but be sure the front rail stays square to the shelf as pressure is applied. ■

for the muntin assembly (see the top right photo on p. 122).

I ripped the muntin stock on the tablesaw and planed and scraped it to its final $\frac{5}{32}$-in. thickness. I cut the tenons on the ends of the muntins with a small dovetail saw and fitted them to the mortises in the back of the door with a file. The half-lap joint where the two muntins cross was done on the tablesaw. After gluing in the muntin assembly and letting it dry, I planed it flush with the front of the door frame.

I cut the glass for the door, but the edges were still a bit ragged, so I cleaned them up on a belt sander clamped into my bench vise. A 100-grit belt eased the edges quickly but safely.

To hold the glass in the rabbet in the back of the door frame, I spot-glued a laminated, curved bar across the top and straight strips against the two sides and the bottom. I made the curved bar from three thin strips, using the top rail as a form and planing them flush after the glue had dried. Because these retaining bars are just glued to the frame in a few spots each, they can be pried out and the glass replaced, if necessary. When the glue had dried, I scraped, sanded and finished the door.

Location of dowel hinge holes is critical

I wanted the door on this clock to swing up rather than out, and I didn't want to mar the clock's appearance with metal hardware. My solution was to pivot the door on two short sections of $\frac{3}{16}$-in.-dia. dowel set into holes in the door's edge and on the inside of the clock case. The exact placement of the holes is critical, but it's not difficult. Before drilling the holes in the sides of the door, I did a test with a piece of scrap the same size as my door. I wanted to be sure the door wouldn't bind on the bottom edge of the front rail when opened and that it would set back $\frac{1}{4}$ in. into the clock case.

To drill the hinge holes in the door, I used a doweling jig and a hand-held drill. I drilled the holes in the case sides on the drill press, shimming the underside of the thinner end to get the sides level.

The dowel I used was a little too fat to fit in the holes I had drilled, so I shaved it with a block plane before cutting it to length—about $\frac{3}{4}$ in. to start.

I dry-fitted the door in the clock case and fine-tuned the length of the dowels with a file until I had an even reveal on both sides of the case, without much play.

Door knob is turned from a blank shaped to a Morse taper The small pull is made of the same wood as the clock case. I first shaped a 1-in.-sq., 3-in.-long piece of pear into a rough Morse taper, leaving about $\frac{3}{4}$ in. at the end for the knob. I cut off the end the drive spurs had bitten into, replaced the drive center with the tapered plug and tapped it securely in place. With the end free, but secure, I turned a small knob. Then I sanded, burnished and finished it right on the lathe before cutting it free from the tapered plug with a small tenon saw.

I marked the location of the knob mortise at the center of the bottom door rail and drilled it on the drill press. After some final fitting of the knob tenon with a file and sandpaper, I glued and clamped the knob to the door using a hand screw.

To hold the door in place when it's closed, I used a $\frac{1}{4}$-in. bullet catch made by Brusso and sold through many woodworking-supply catalogs. The Brusso catch is the cleanest, smallest and least intrusive one I've seen.

I dry-assembled the clock, with the door in place. The door is positioned correctly when it is set back from the front edge of the case by $\frac{1}{4}$ in. evenly top to bottom. I marked straight down from the front edge of the door at its center. Then I located the center of the bottom part of the bullet catch $\frac{5}{16}$ in. back from that mark. I centered the top part of the catch on the $\frac{5}{8}$-in.-thick door. The hole in the door can be bored freehand. But I drilled the hole in the bottom shelf on a drill press. Both pieces of the bullet catch can be pushed in place. No glue is needed.

A TEMPLATE AND GUIDE SHAPE THE TOP DOOR RAIL. After bandsawing the curve in the rail to rough shape, the author routs it to finished shape.

MUNTINS ARE TENONED INTO OPEN MORTISES IN FRAME. Tap the tenons home with a small hammer and a wooden block.

BACK VIEW OF DOOR

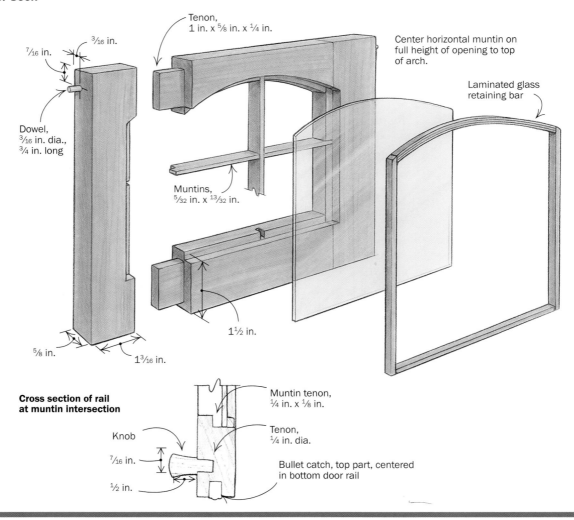

Tenon,
1 in. x 5/8 in. x 1/4 in.

Center horizontal muntin on full height of opening to top of arch.

Laminated glass retaining bar

3/16 in.

7/16 in.

Dowel,
3/16 in. dia.,
3/4 in. long

Muntins,
5/32 in. x 13/32 in.

1 1/2 in.

5/8 in.

1 3/16 in.

Cross section of rail at muntin intersection

Muntin tenon,
1/4 in. x 1/8 in.

Tenon,
1/4 in. dia.

Knob

7/16 in.

1/2 in.

Bullet catch, top part, centered in bottom door rail

ASSEMBLE CASE ON ITS SIDE

I laid one side of the case on the workbench and glued in the bottom and middle shelves. Next I slid in the veneered face panel with the works attached. I set in the completed door and then carefully lowered the other case side, lining up all the mating parts. After standing the clock upright, I glued the top on and clamped up the whole assembly, side to side and top to bottom. I adjusted the clamps until the case was square (see the photo at right). The back of the clock, which slides home in a groove, goes on last.

After the glue had dried, I cut, planed and finished one side of a ¼-in.-thick door stop. I glued the door stop onto the bottom shelf, using spring clamps to hold it in place until the glue had set. The bullet catch provides a positive stop for the door, but the door stop will prevent the door from being inadvertently jammed past the catch, possibly breaking the hinge dowels or the case itself.

SNAP PENDULUM ROD TO SIZE, AND ATTACH HANDS

The pendulum hanger extends down into the lower compartment through the cutout in the middle shelf. The hanger supports the adjustable pendulum shaft. The pendulum shaft is manufactured with scored lines across its back so that it can be broken to length. I broke off the shaft so the center of the pendulum bob would swing past the cross hairs formed by the muntins of the door.

I positioned the one-piece dial and bezel over the clock stem extending through the veneered face panel (the dial is the face of the clock; the bezel is the brass-bound glass disc). Then I fastened the dial with a thin brass nut. I press-fitted the hands over the stem and screwed on the top nut. Each hand has a slot or hole that corresponds with a portion of the dial stem. Next I tacked the dial in place with the eight tiny brads that came with it. Once the dial was tacked down, I put in a D battery and turned on the clock.

Finally, I turned the clock upside down (after temporarily removing the pendulum shaft and bob) and slid the back of the case in from the bottom. I secured it with two ¾-in. #8 brass screws driven into the back edge of the bottom shelf. The removable back makes it easy to change the battery or turn off the clock.

ASSEMBLE THE CLOCK ON ITS SIDE, turn it upright and then place the top on the clock. Adjust the clamps as necessary to make the case square.

SOURCES OF SUPPLY

The quartz Bim-Bam movement and the dial-bezel combination are from Merritt's Antiques (P.O. Box 277, Douglassville, PA 19518-0277; 800-345-4101). The movement is part #P-647W/P and costs $39.50. The dial-bezel combination is part #P-222 and costs $16.75.

The hands are from S. LaRose (3223 Yanceyville St., P.O. Box 21208, Greensboro, NC 27420; 336-621-1936). The hands are part #816012 and cost 75¢. ■

MARIO RODRIGUEZ

A Mantel with a Mission

Some friends of mine live in an attractive but indistinguishable Ranch-style house. Built in the 1970s, it's a typical tract house, produced cookie-cutter style to fit a tight budget and a streamlined modern lifestyle. They loved the house when they bought it, but they always knew there were a few things they would want to improve. First on their list was to do something with the plain brick fireplace and raised hearth in the living room.

When they came to me looking for a nice wooden mantel, it took some time to find a design that matched the house, the furnishings and the owners' tastes all at the same time. The raised hearth was originally intended to make a cozy fireplace perch. A nice idea, but it brought up a design problem I've never had to deal with before: Exactly what kind of mantel do you install on a raised hearth fireplace?

After looking through a number of books and a lot of experimenting at the sketch board, I decided a simple wraparound mantel in an Arts-and-Crafts style would work nicely. A wrap-around mantel would enhance the horizontal sweep of masonry, not fight with it. I also considered ease of construction and time and materials. With a little planning, I'd be able to construct the majority of the mantel in my own shop and install the whole job with only a day's work in my friends' living room.

The design I settled on calls for a simple four-panel overmantel and a 2¼-in.-thick

mantel shelf. I wanted the mantel to appear well-balanced and symmetrical, so I designed the shelf to rest on five brackets that are all directly in line with the stiles on the overmantel.

A bluestone slab on top of the hearth would be an attractive way to cover the brick, and a wooden skirt around the raised hearth would hide the masonry, tying the hearth and mantel together visually. I didn't want anything to detract from the design or distract the viewer, so I chose rift-cut red oak, both solid and plywood. This combined the rich, rough surface of oak with an inconspicuous dead-straight grain.

I was able to speed the construction process by doing most of the work in my own shop and reducing the number of cuts I had to make for the joinery (see the photos on p. 126). I used plywood with a solid frame to make up the four-panel overmantel. For the rails and stiles, I used ¾-in.-thick red oak, milled with a ¼-in. plow, ¾ in. deep and centered on the inside edges of the frame. This one groove acted as both a mortise for the stub tenons and as the groove to hold the panels.

For the ¾-in. stub tenons on the ends of the rails and short stiles, I used a tablesaw to cut the shoulders and a bandsaw to cut the cheeks. Then I installed a dado blade on the tablesaw to cut rabbets into the ½-in.-thick plywood panels. All the joinery was cut with only a few machine setups. The frame-and-panel overmantel slipped easily together for

Quick frame-and-panel joinery

SINGLE GROOVE DOES DOUBLE DUTY. A groove plowed with a dado blade serves as both the mortise for the tenons and the groove to hold the panel.

STUB TENONS MAKE IT PLENTY STRONG. With the shoulders cut on a tablesaw, a bandsaw completes the stub tenons on the ends of the rails and short stiles.

FAST RABBETS WITH A DADO BLADE. The panels are rabbeted with a dado blade. The frame-and-panel overmantel is glued up before it leaves the shop. ∎

glue-up in the shop. The plywood returns were mitered to the end stiles for a cleaner, more seamless look. I used biscuits to align and secure them in place.

A Plywood Mantel Shelf Is Lightweight

If I had used a 2¼-in. slab of solid red oak for the shelf, it would have added considerable weight. Instead, I used two layers of ¾-in. red-oak plywood with ¾-in. plywood strips as spacers. The use of plywood also eliminated cross-grain movement or shrinkage, which could be considerable so near a source of heat.

I cut two identical pieces to make up the top and bottom of the shelf. One of the spacers is placed flush with the front of the shelf; the other is inset ½ in. from the back. Leaving this room on the back edge reduced the amount of material I'd have to trim to get a snug fit when the shelf was installed.

With the shelf built up to a thickness of 2¼ in., I glued plywood spacers on each of the returns that extend back to the wall. When the shelf was dry, I edged the entire lamination with red oak cut to a light ⅛ in. thick on the tablesaw. When the glue had dried, the overhang was carefully trimmed flush to the plywood with a block plane, then scraped and sanded.

Cut Everything Ahead of Time

The mantel skirt is made of ¾-in. red-oak plywood, mitered at the outside corners and later nailed into place. I prepared the wood for the mantel skirt, but I did not assemble it in the shop. By leaving the skirt in parts, I could easily scribe the returns to the wall before they were attached.

I knew that there would probably be a conspicuous gap between the masonry and the skirt's bottom edge. I also knew that the exposed plywood edge of the skirt would have to be covered. A simple and attractive way to deal with both problems was to attach a quirk-and-bead molding along the bottom edge of the mantel skirt. I used a ¾-in. beading bit to run off two 8-ft. pieces from clean, straight-grained oak. This allowed me a little more than I'd need.

For the cornice molding, I used a simple 1⅝-in. cove molding from a local lumberyard. This type of molding is usually a stock profile and shouldn't be difficult to find.

Because of their prominent position, the brackets on this mantel must be well executed: clean square edges and smooth flowing curves. Aside from the installation, they're probably the most demanding part of this job. The method I use ensures crisp edges and reliable curves (see the photos on p. 130).

The skirt around the hearth does more than just cover the bricks: It's the key to connecting the hearth and mantel visually. The hearth skirt is also made of ¾-in.-thick red-oak plywood mitered at the corners and tacked over cleats that are screwed to the brick. With the plywood for the hearth skirt cut to size, my work in the shop was almost done.

FINISH BEFORE MANTEL IS ATTACHED TO THE WALL

Finishing can be a slow and tedious process if you wait until the whole piece is assembled and installed. The process goes much faster when things can be laid out flat in your own shop before you have to be careful with someone else's walls.

After all the parts were sanded with 220-grit paper, I applied a light honey-colored oil-based stain by Minwax (Ipswich pine) with a 2-in. brush and wiped up drips with a rag. When the stain was dry, I coated all the parts with two light coats of orange shellac. This gives the oak a very rich color with a slight orange cast. If your taste runs to a cooler shade of oak, you can use blond shellac instead of orange. To get a satin finish, I gently rubbed out the shellac with steel wool between coats.

Rubbing out woodwork usually results in cut-throughs—spots on the sharp outside corners where the color and finish have been rubbed through by the steel wool. To repair these spots, I ran a medium-brown furniture marker along the exposed edges, quickly blending them in. The mantel could be installed and this finish left alone, but by applying a glaze after installation, you see a real transformation in the room (see the box on p. 131).

TAP-CON SCREWS MAKE INSTALLATION EASY

With most of my work already done, the mantel went into place quicker than I thought it would. Figuring that the top

■ Preparation is key to success

STARTING FROM SCRATCH. To make this design work, the area above the fireplace was built out flush with the brick. A 2x4 frame was attached above the fireplace; drywall and mud made it a workable wall. All the stud positions were marked, and measurements were taken to make sure the mantel went up without a hitch. ■

surface of the mantel shelf should be about 53 in. from the floor, I marked the wall to help me place the overmantel's bottom edge. Along the top edge of the overmantel, I screwed a strip of ¾-in. plywood. The strip allows me to use a narrower top rail and limits cross-grain movement at the joint. The plywood strip will also flex, so there is no strain or pressure on the solid top rail when the overmantel goes onto the wall.

Next I centered the brackets under the overmantel stiles and attached each with a single countersunk lag bolt from behind (see the top right photo on p. 130). A single bolt will secure the brackets to the mantel skirt but will still allow them to be pivoted slightly.

Hanging the mantel skirt is a critical step in the installation. If the skirt doesn't go up perfectly plumb and level, the shelf will have either a forward or backward pitch. I inserted shims behind the skirt and directly underneath each bracket to ensure that the placement was just right. With the brackets pivoted out of the way, a few Tap-Con screws tied the whole unit into the wall.

OVERMANTEL SLIDES ONTO THE WALL. With the overmantel shimmed level, driving a few screws ties it to the wall.

SKIRT ABUTS THE OVER-MANTEL. Shims guarantee that the overmantel and skirt meet flush.

SHELF FITS EASILY ONTO THE BRACKETS. Using reliable measurements in the planning stage ensures the shelf seats itself perfectly level. ■

This mantel was designed to revive an old fireplace with a raised hearth. The use of a straight-grained wood draws attention to the design. Small details like a repeated cornice molding tie the hearth and overmantel together visually.

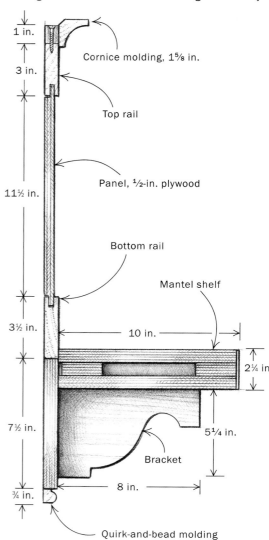

1 in.

3 in.

Cornice molding, 1⅝ in.

Top rail

11½ in.

Panel, ½-in. plywood

Bottom rail

Mantel shelf

3½ in.

10 in.

2¼ in.

7½ in.

5¼ in.

Bracket

¾ in.

8 in.

Quirk-and-bead molding

Those Tap-Con masonry screws were key to a simple installation. I've used the bright blue screws before on another mantel installation and was surprised at the simple two-step procedure. Instead of using lead or plastic anchors, Tap-Con screws only require one simple pre-drilled hole before driving the screws home. Once home, they hold tight, and nothing short of a pry bar will loosen them. But they can be easily withdrawn with a screw gun if something has to be repositioned or removed.

I snugged the tip of the ¾-in. plywood skirt to the bottom edge of the overmantel and secured it with four Tap-Con screws. These screws are hidden when the mantel shelf is in place. I made sure the brackets were all level and ran a screw diagonally from the top of the brackets into the mantel skirt to give them extra strength.

The shelf was designed to extend 5 in. beyond the corner of the overmantel and 10 in. from the overmantel face. It should fit without much trouble around the overmantel

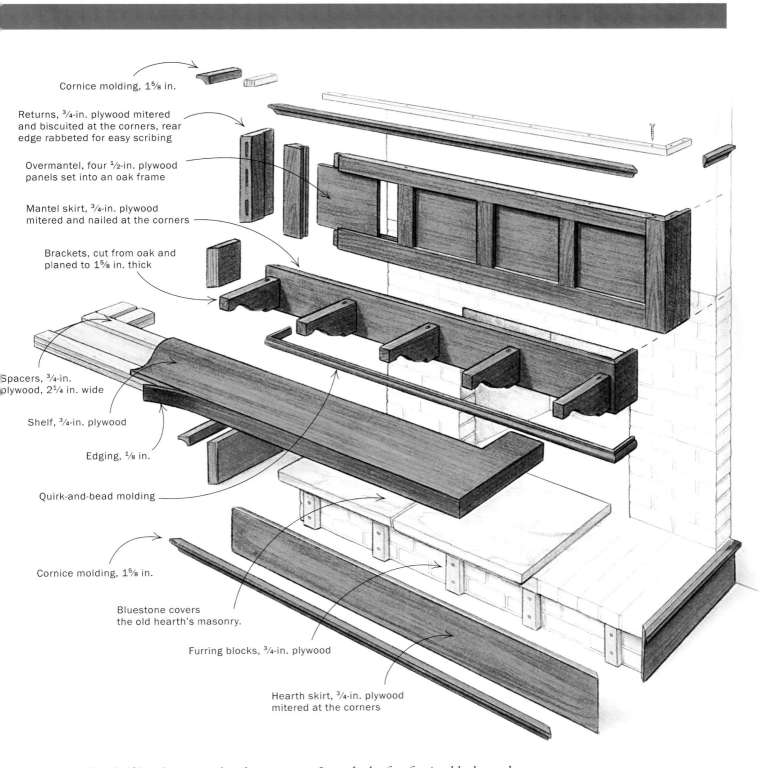

Cornice molding, 1⅝ in.

Returns, ¾-in. plywood mitered
and biscuited at the corners, rear
edge rabbeted for easy scribing

Overmantel, four ½-in. plywood
panels set into an oak frame

Mantel skirt, ¾-in. plywood
mitered and nailed at the corners

Brackets, cut from oak and
planed to 1⅝ in. thick

Spacers, ¾-in.
plywood, 2¼ in. wide

Shelf, ¾-in. plywood

Edging, ⅛ in.

Quirk-and-bead molding

Cornice molding, 1⅝ in.

Bluestone covers
the old hearth's masonry.

Furring blocks, ¾-in. plywood

Hearth skirt, ¾-in. plywood
mitered at the corners

and onto the shelf brackets. I used a plane
and a 2-in. chisel to trim the inside of the
shelf for a snug fit against a wall that wasn't
completely square. A few 1½-in. #8 screws
driven through the bottom side of the
bracket were used to hold the shelf tight.

I attached a few furring blocks to the
hearth's masonry with Tap-Con screws so
that I'd be able to nail the skirt in place.
The ¾-in. plywood skirt had already been
mitered and cut to the right width in the
shop, so I only had to make sure everything

■ Brackets with perfect curves

THE EYE NOTICES WHEN A CURVE IS NOT EXACTLY CIRCULAR. Using a Forstner bit gives the author a true and reliable curve.

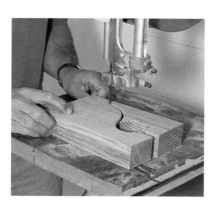

A TABLESAW KEEPS THE EDGES SQUARE. A tablesaw and a crosscut box are used for an exact cut on the bracket's square ends.

A FRESH BLADE AND A STEADY HAND. The rest of the outline is finished on a bandsaw fitted with a fresh ¼-in. 6-tpi blade. After completing the outline of the brackets, a series of rasps, files, scrapers and sandpaper produces a smooth surface free of any machine marks. ■

■ Installing the brackets

A SINGLE LAG BOLT SECURES A BRACKET IN PLACE. With the bracket clamped at a perfect right angle to the skirt, the author has two free hands to secure a lag bolt from behind.

fit. I trimmed the ends of the returns with a jigsaw to get a tight fit against the molding on the wall. Glue and a pneumatic nail gun with 1¼-in. finish nails secured everything.

Applying the molding made the whole thing come together. I used the same molding at the top of the overmantel as I did at the top of the hearth skirt, so everything looked natural and seemed to belong. I cut miters for all the molding on a power miter box at the site, and then I nailed it into place with my pneumatic gun. Later, the nail holes were filled with a dark wax. I also ran a bead of caulk between the masonry and the mantel skirt to make sure no stray sparks could get trapped.

With all the parts pre-finished, I applied a quick glazing to knock off the high shine and give the mantel a subtle, mature look (see the box on the facing page). When the stone was placed on the skirt as a final touch, the mantel seemed to have been ripped out of a Frank Lloyd Wright home and installed in my friend's living room. The only thing left to do was build a fire.

THE BRACKETS TWIST AWAY. When the skirt slides over the brick, the lag bolts allow the author to twist the brackets for easy access to a hidden spot to sink a screw.

A SCREW LOCKS THE BRACKET. After the skirt is tied to the wall, a screw is driven at 45° to hold the bracket permanently in place.

SHELF IS ATTACHED FROM UNDERNEATH. The shelf goes onto the brackets, and an inconspicuously placed screw keeps it there. ■

■ AN AGED LOOK THAT DOESN'T TAKE 50 YEARS

With a glazing gel, I can make the mantel look either slightly old or very old. I start with McCloskey's glaze and stir in a raw umber Japan color until I get an almost chocolate color with a yogurt consistency.

I paint a thick coat in the spots that I want darkest: the recesses and the areas where stray smoke would have inevitably darkened the wood over time. But I barely touch the parts I want to stay light.

I let that dry a few minutes, apply another coat if necessary and start pulling off the glaze with a piece of cheesecloth or an old T-shirt. If a spot looks too dark, a little paint thinner on a rag will pull it up.

I leave it dark in the crannies where furniture polish, oils and dust would have accumulated with age.

When I'm happy with the shading on the mantel, I wipe it quickly one last time, using a rag and a tiny bit of thinner.

After a few days of drying, a light coat of shellac or wax will tie down the glaze. This painless process subdues the mantel and conjures an aged, smoky appearance that seems natural in the room.

PATRICK NELSON

Stickley-Style Legs

Quartersawn oak is synonymous with Craftsman furniture. The wood's wild ray figure is both beautiful and distinctive. Unfortunately, Mother Nature saw fit to put it only on opposing faces of a board. So on a table leg, for example, the sides adjacent to a quartersawn face should be flatsawn and without figure.

However, if you look closely at much of the furniture built by the Stickleys in the early 1900s, you'll see what looks like a freak of nature: quartersawn figure on all four sides of square table legs (see the photo at left). This figure is the result of a unique leg design used in Stickley factories.

The Stickleys used two techniques. One was to cover the flatsawn faces with quartersawn veneer. The other technique mated four quartersawn boards with trapezoidal profiles. The base of each trapezoid was one face of the leg, and the two adjacent sides were angled at 45°. On one angled side, there was a small perpendicular notch; on the other side was a complementary tooth. Mating tooth to notch on adjacent pieces lined up the four joints perfectly.

■ Quartersawn Figure on All Four Sides

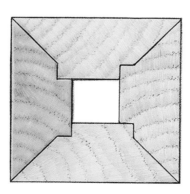

STICKLEY METHOD

On original Stickley pieces, the leg was made up of four pieces. Each of these pieces had two complementary profiles cut into it using two shaper setups.

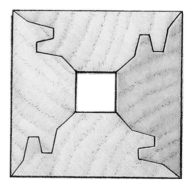

AUTHOR'S VERSION

The author's version of the Stickley leg is made up of four identical pieces. The edge profile on each piece mates with the face profile on an adjacent piece.

FREAK OF NATURE? No, just a bit of technical wizardry. Quartersawn figure occurs naturally only on opposing faces of a board, but the legs on many Craftsman pieces show it all around. The author used one router bit and two jigs to make the leg shown at left.

First Jig, First Pass

One jig positions workpiece flat on table to cut the profile on edge of stock.

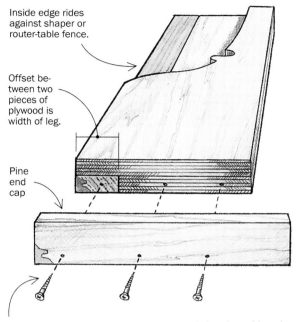

Inside edge rides against shaper or router-table fence.

Offset between two pieces of plywood is width of leg.

Pine end cap

Screws hold end cap in place. Screw in workpiece is positioned out of the way of the bit.

ROUT THE EDGE PROFILE FIRST. Maintain a steady feed rate, and keep pressure against the fence. Each profile is cut in a single pass.

Second Jig, Second Pass

Second jig positions workpiece vertically to cut the profile on the inside face.

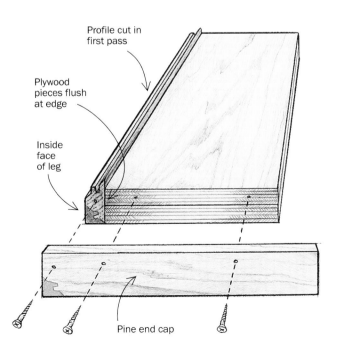

Profile cut in first pass

Plywood pieces flush at edge

Inside face of leg

Pine end cap

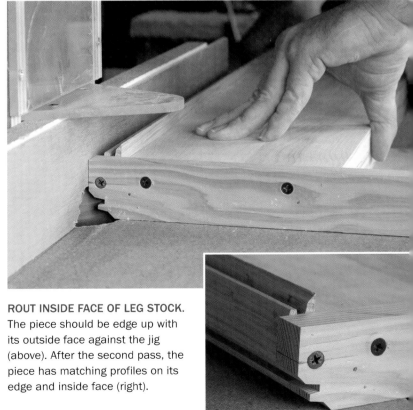

ROUT INSIDE FACE OF LEG STOCK. The piece should be edge up with its outside face against the jig (above). After the second pass, the piece has matching profiles on its edge and inside face (right).

1. Apply glue to just two pieces of each leg at a time. Then, after you have the two halves assembled, apply glue to the remaining faces, and bring the two halves together.

2. Tack battens down center of each side. These battens will help concentrate the clamping pressure.

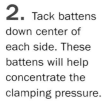

3. Tack one end of a bungee cord to the end of a batten.

4. Wrap cord tightly around the assembly. Tack the bungee cord at the other end.

ONE MODERN BIT DOES THE TRICK

The shaper bits used to mill the original Stickley design are not commonly available today, but the widely available lock-miter router bit can be used to make these Stickley-style legs. The bit is beveled at 45°, like a large chamfer bit, with a pair of opposing teeth in the middle of the cutting surface. It cuts a profile that's quite similar to the one used by the Stickleys. I bought my bit from Grizzly Imports (P.O. Box 2069, Bellingham, WA 98227; 800-541-

5537). They're also sold by a number of other router-bit manufacturers.

The lock-miter bit actually has some advantages over the shaper cutters used by the Stickleys: This bit produces a joint with a larger glue-surface area, only one is needed to cut both sides of the joint, and just one setup is required. Adjusting the lock-miter bit height and the position of the fence to get that setting is just trial-and-error. You can get pretty close right from the start, though, by centering one of the teeth on the stock. And once you have the setting right, the actual routing takes just a few minutes.

5. Tap along the battens to make sure the joints are seated.

6. The wrapped assembly is set aside to let the glue cure. After a few hours, the leg can be unwrapped and the ends trimmed. This eliminates the screw holes and any slight gaps at the ends where the clamping pressure isn't as great. The leg is now ready to use. ■

I mount the bit in my shaper rather than in a router table. The shaper's slower speed is less intimidating than a router with a bit of this size. But if you don't have a shaper, the technique would work using a powerful, variable-speed router set at its slowest speed. The key to the technique is the pair of jigs I made to hold the workpieces as they're fed through the bit (see the drawings on p. 133).

One Jig for Each Pass

The first jig holds the workpiece flat against the table and exposes the edge of the work-piece to the router. The jig is made of two pieces of plywood with pine end caps. The end caps start out as rectangular pieces but take on the lock-miter profile after the first pass. Screws driven through the end caps, far enough back to be out of the bit's way, hold the workpiece in place (see the top drawing on p. 133). The distance from the edge of the narrower piece of plywood, against which the workpiece butts, to the edge of the wider piece, which rides against the fence, is the width of the leg. It's easy to make the legs any size you want.

Stock from $\frac{9}{16}$ in. thick on up to 1 in. or $1\frac{1}{4}$ in. (depending on the make of the bit) can be used with the lock-miter bit, but the thickness of the parts of the jig and the stock you're using for the pieces that will make up the leg must be identical. I dimensioned stock to the thickness of the shop-grade plywood (nominally $\frac{3}{4}$ in.) that I used for the jig. It was easier than building up each layer of the jig from multiple pieces of plywood or milling the pieces of the jig from solid wood. I also crosscut the leg stock and jig stock at the same time, so their lengths are identical.

The second jig looks similar to the first one. But the two pieces of plywood are the same size, and they are flush on their edges (see the bottom drawing on p. 133). The workpiece is held vertically against the edges of the plywood. This way, the inner face of the workpiece is presented to the router bit.

After the workpiece has passed through the router bit in this second jig, the workpiece will have identical profiles on one edge and on the inside face. Each leg is made up of four such pieces, one edge of each piece mating with the face of the adjacent piece, all the way around the leg. I always make the legs several inches longer than they will be on the finished piece of furniture so that I can trim off the ends after the leg has been assembled.

These legs can be used on many different kinds of furniture, and the process of making a leg is the same, regardless of size or what the leg will be used for.

KEVIN P. RODEL

Fuming with Ammonia

Anyone who's spent time mucking out stables, or just walking through a working barn, knows how pungent ammonia fumes are. Those fumes have darkened the beams of many a barn over the centuries. I wouldn't doubt that many farmers put two and two together when they noticed how quickly oak acquired an aged patina.

Around the turn of the century, fuming became popular with many of the furnituremakers and manufacturers working in the Arts-and-Crafts style. So much so that when most people think of Stickley, Limbert or Roycroft furniture, fumed white oak is what they see in their mind's eye.

Other woods can be fumed, but white oak responds best and most predictably to fuming (see the top photos on p. 138). For a look at the effects of fuming on other woods, see the box on p. 139.

Regardless of species, boards that will be fumed should all come from one tree. Different trees within a species will vary in their tannin content because of growing conditions. This will affect how they react to the ammonia. Because it's difficult to get boards all from one tree at a regular lumberyard, I buy most of my lumber from specialty dealers who saw their own.

FUMING WITH AMMONIA gives white oak that classic golden-brown color. Before it's been fumed (inset), white oak is a pale, almost cool, tan.

I began fuming furniture because I'd become increasingly interested in the Arts-and-Crafts movement. I had been making more furniture in that tradition, and I wanted it to convey the look and feel of the originals. The finish seemed like an important element in the whole equation. Fuming is not the perfect colorant for every situation and wood species, but where it does work, it works very well and can give a superior finish to stains or dyes.

Stains obscure the surface of the wood somewhat. Worse yet, on ring-porous woods like oak, pigments collect in large open pores, making the rings very dark and overly pronounced. The effect is quite unnatural and looks to me like thousands of dark specks sprinkled across the surface. Also, stains are time-consuming to apply, and I have a strong aversion to exposing myself to the volatile fumes of the petroleum-based products found in most commercial stains.

Aniline dyes do a better job than stains, but they're also rather labor-intensive and can be very tricky to apply well. Dyes also fade over time, especially in direct sunlight. Fumed wood is colorfast.

The thing I like best about fuming is that what you see after the process is still only the wood, just as clearly as before. It's just darker. That's because the ammonia reacts with tannins that are naturally present in the wood, actually changing the color of the wood, not merely adding a superficial layer of color. Samples of fumed wood that I've cut open show a ragged line of darker wood between $\frac{1}{16}$ in. and $\frac{1}{8}$ in. deep.

Another thing I like about fuming is that it's virtually foolproof. The first piece you fume will look great. Unlike stains or dyes, fuming won't make a piece look blotchy or cause drips. And there's one other benefit to fuming. While the piece of furniture is being fumed, you can get back to work. The ammonia keeps working while you're taking care of other business.

HANDLE AMMONIA WITH CARE

The first and most important consideration when fuming is safety. Before you even buy

AQUEOUS AMMONIA IS POURED INTO A GLASS CONTAINER placed at the bottom of the fuming chamber (left). Then the top of the chamber is lowered quickly onto its base (above). Protective gear is essential.

the ammonia, make sure you have a properly fitted face-mask respirator with ammonia-filtering cartridges. Other types of cartridges, such as those used for spraying lacquer or other finishes, are not designed to filter ammonia fumes and will not offer protection. Ammonia cartridges are inexpensive and available at any fire or safety equipment store. Look in the yellow pages for the one nearest you.

Eye protection is essential. I use swimming goggles, which fit tightly around the eyes. The purpose of the goggles is to protect the eyes from fumes, not just accidental splashes. Rubber or plastic gloves are also necessary. Read the precautions on the side of the ammonia bottle, too.

Finally, if you're trying this for the first time and you work in a basement shop, wait until the weather is nice and do the fuming outside. After you become comfortable with the procedure, you can consider doing it indoors.

The reason for all the precautions when fuming is that ammonia used for fuming wood is not common household ammonia. It is a strong aqueous solution that has between 26% and 30% ammonium hydroxide. Household ammonia has less than 5%.

You'll want to buy the ammonia locally and pick it up yourself. Because it is considered a hazardous substance, shipping charges are high (more than the cost of the ammonia). This industrial-strength ammonia is used in machines that reproduce blueprints and surveys, so you can usually find it at business-supply, blueprint-supply or

Unfinished				
Oil finish				
Unfumed	One-half hour	2 hours	8 hours	32 hours

surveyor-supply stores (look in the yellow pages for a supplier). It's sold by the gallon. Here in Maine, it costs between $6 and $10. And 1 gal. fumes a lot of furniture.

BRINGING AMMONIA AND WOOD TOGETHER

With safety equipment and ammonia in hand, you're almost ready to fume. All you need now is some kind of fuming chamber—the more airtight the better. The most versatile and efficient chamber construction seems to be a heavy-gauge (3 mil or greater) plastic wrap stapled to a simple softwood frame that's held together with drywall screws (see the top right photo on p. 137).

This type of chamber is lightweight, can be made to just about any size and can be broken down into flat panels for storage. If a fairly large chamber is needed, one side panel can be used as a detachable doorway. Use spring clamps or hand screws to attach the door panel and felt weather stripping as a gasket to seal the chamber. Small chambers can be placed over the items being fumed, as in the photo at right above. If you're fuming outdoors, be sure to weight or tie down this kind of chamber. They're very light and blow over easily.

I've used many other types of fuming chambers as well—everything from large plastic trash cans (perfect for small items) to a rented moving van. The van allowed me to fume an entire bedroom set at one time for a reasonable cost. The ammonia did no harm to the van, and by the time I returned it the morning after fuming, there was little if any residual smell. And because every

piece was exposed to the ammonia for the same amount of time, I was able to achieve a precise color match.

Prepare a piece of furniture to be fumed the same way you would for staining or finishing. Scrape or sand until the surface is smooth, and remove any hardware. Place the piece of furniture in the chamber so that no part that will be visible is touching anything. If the ammonia vapors can't circulate, they won't be able to react with the tannins in the wood. As a result, that spot will not darken like the rest of the piece.

Never let the furniture come into direct contact with the aqueous ammonia because it is very corrosive. I use glass pie plates to hold the ammonia. They're relatively inexpensive, clean up completely and can be used over and over again. They also present a large surface area to the air so the ammonia evaporates readily.

I fill a plate about half full and place it on the floor of the chamber (see the photo at left on p. 137). The plate should be filled quickly but carefully. If you're fuming a particularly large piece or more than one piece, you may want to use two or three pie plates. Attach the door to the chamber, or lower the chamber onto its base. With the fumes confined to the chamber, you can remove your mask and goggles. Note the time so you can keep track of the exposure.

TEST PIECES DETERMINE COLOR

The length of time a given piece will need to be fumed depends on the volume of the chamber, the amount of ammonia used, the species of wood being fumed and the depth of color you're looking for. Knowing when to remove a piece is largely a matter of personal experience. You can hedge your bets, though.

The best way to know when you have achieved the desired amount of fuming is to use test pieces. I always place three or four pieces of scrap, preferably cutoffs from the same project, on the floor of the chamber. When I think enough time has gone by, I don mask and goggles, quickly open the chamber, remove one of the scrap pieces and reseal the chamber.

When it first comes out of the chamber, the wood will have a gray, almost weathered, look. Don't be alarmed; this is normal. To see an approximation of what the finished piece will look like, I apply a coat of finish. As soon as the finish goes on, the real color imparted by the fuming appears instantly, almost magically. If I want the piece darker, I'll continue checking the color of the scrap boards at regular intervals until I'm happy with the result.

If, after eight hours in the chamber, a piece is still lighter than you'd like, you should replace the ammonia. I put on my mask, goggles and gloves, open the chamber and dump the old ammonia into a bucket of water. I add fresh ammonia to the pie plate, reseal the chamber and leave the bucket of diluted ammonia outside for a day. Then I pour it around the trees in our orchard or on the compost heap.

Once you've decided the wood is dark enough, remove it from the chamber, and let the piece of furniture off-gas for eight to 12 hours. I try to plan my fuming sessions so that the piece comes out of the chamber at the end of the work day. By morning, there's little residual smell.

At this point, you can apply your finish. Oil, varnish, shellac—any finish will work. There's no problem with compatibility between a piece of furniture that's been fumed and the topcoat. At the same time, fuming doesn't protect the surface of a piece in any way, so build up your finish as you would normally.

■ FUMING COMMON FURNITURE WOODS

The practice of fuming wood to enhance its color is most often associated with white oak. The oaks in general are high in tannin and fume well, though red oak tends to turn greenish rather than deep brown like white oak. Other species contain varying amounts of tannins and can be fumed, but the effects are generally not as pronounced as with white oak. I was curious about the effects of fuming on other furniture woods, so I fumed a number of them for four hours.

I'd heard that nontannic woods could be fumed if a solution of tannic acid was applied to the surface of the wood first, so I tried that as well. (Tannic acid is available from Olde Mill Cabinet Shoppe; 717-755-8884.) Tannic acid is sold as a powder that you add to water. I added tannic acid to a pint of water until the solution was saturated, applied the solution with a foam brush and then let the samples dry overnight before fuming. Here are the results.

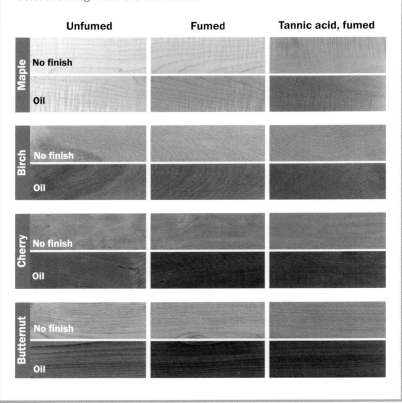

My preferred finish has always been boiled linseed oil (I use Tried and True brand because it builds quickly and contains no metal driers). Three or four coats over fumed oak impart a subtle amber overtone that's in keeping with the look of Arts-and-Crafts furniture.

Inspiration

Your workshop is a creative outlet. Sometimes you want to make simple projects, sometimes elaborate, and sometimes you're just not sure. That's where this section comes in. You'll find a variety of examples here to inspire you. Specifications and design information help you make the leap from inspiration to reality.

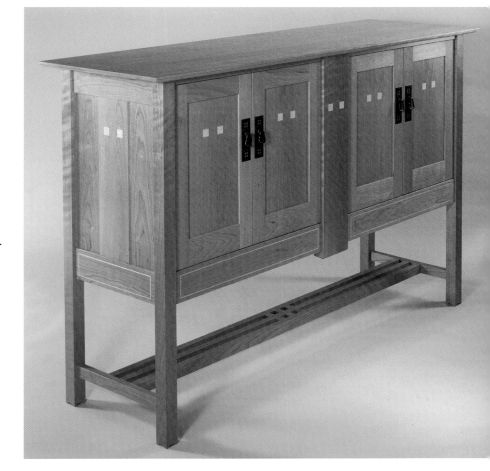

DAVE SIGMAN

Morris Chair

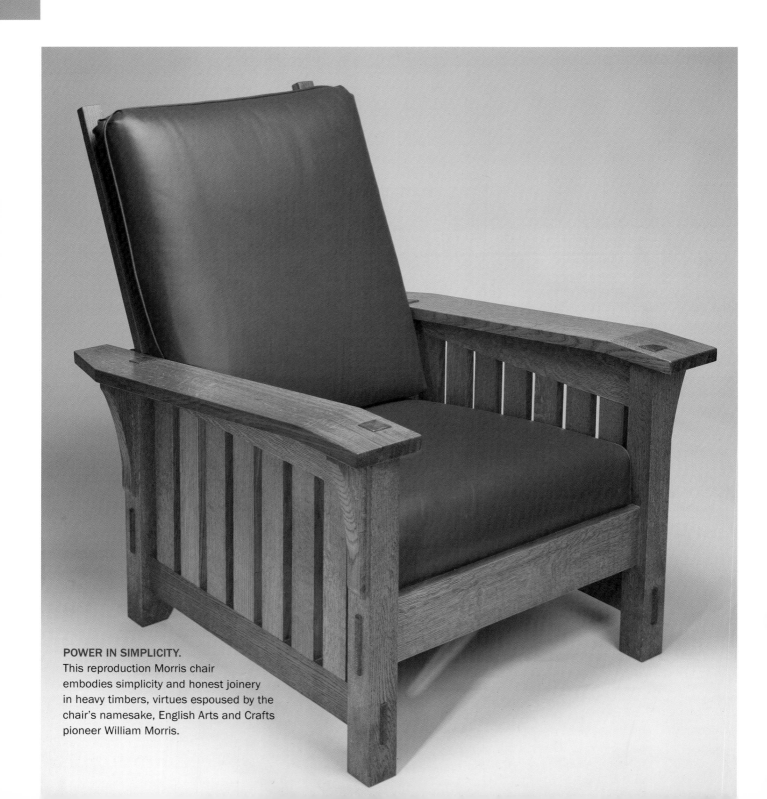

POWER IN SIMPLICITY.
This reproduction Morris chair
embodies simplicity and honest joinery
in heavy timbers, virtues espoused by the
chair's namesake, English Arts and Crafts
pioneer William Morris.

I was first exposed to Mission style furniture about 10 years ago and was immediately struck by the beauty and simplicity of it. Most appealing to me was Gustav Stickley's reclining Morris chair. A massive yet graceful piece of furniture, it is a prime example of Stickley's beliefs that art should be found in the objects we use every day and that ornamentation and function should work together.

After studying pictures and articles, as well as a few authentic pieces, I set about building one for myself. The chair's pleasures are simple: stout construction, elemental forms left unadorned. It seemed to me that the quality of the materials and the way they were handled were paramount. I chose quartersawn white oak and heavy leather.

The prominent through-tenons give the chair great strength and are a pleasure to see and touch. Where the tenons came through, I sanded the end grain carefully and gave it plenty of finish to make it gleam.

The chair has become a real focal point in my living room. It is easy to unwind surrounded by the chair's mass, with a good book and a hot cup of tea at the end of a busy day.

A PLACE TO UNWIND. With its sloped arms, reclining back and thick cushions, the Morris chair is built for comfort. A simple system of pegs provides three settings for the back.

SEDUCTIVE STRENGTH. The author lavished attention on the fit and polish of the through-tenons, details that provide strength and satisfaction in a Gustav Stickley piece.

SPECIFICATIONS

■ DIMENSIONS
33 in. wide, 38 in. deep, and 38 in. high.

■ MATERIALS
Quartersawn white oak and leather.

■ FINISH
Dark Walnut Watco Danish Oil and lacquer.

B. A. HARRINGTON

Stickley Prairie Settle

GREAT PLAINS IN OAK. This reproduction of a settle originally made by L. and J. G. Stickley is designed in the Mission style but also evokes the long horizon of the Frank Lloyd Wright-inspired Prairie style.

lthough L. and J. G. are not the most famous of the Stickley brothers, I think they turned out one of the more elegant and handsome oak pieces in the Mission style. Where Gustav Stickley had the wonderful inlay designs of Harvey Ellis to enhance his work, L. and J. G. turned to Frank Lloyd Wright and the Prairie School architects for inspiration. The design for their Prairie settle was based on the settle in Wright's Robie House in Chicago. It has been suggested that no other piece illustrates so well the way this furniture evokes the prairie, with its long horizon.

I have always been drawn to Mission oak furniture because of the heavy, low, stayed-to-the-earth feel it gives. But I was somewhat hesitant when some friends asked me to build a Prairie settle and to give it a finish that would match their other Arts and Crafts furniture. I came to furniture making with a background in art, intent on designing my own pieces, and I was worried that a reproduction would fail to satisfy my creative impulses. I did, however, want to make something for my friends, and I found the piece very attractive. So I agreed.

When I began milling all that quartersawn white oak and saw the spectacular

figure, I realized that my initial worries about finding the project aesthetically unsatisfying had been misplaced. (For details about making the quartersawn posts, see the box on p. 146.) The play between the distinct patterns that emerged and the random action of the rays created a surface of excited movement, which I found I could manipulate by strategically arranging the boards. This led me to see the piece in a new way. Its massive flat surfaces combine to act as a canvas for the rays to move around on, illustrating the appropriateness of quartersawn white oak for this simple and spare style of furniture.

RAYS OF THE GRAIN. The author found that the large flat surfaces of the Mission-style settle provided a stage for the excited movement of the figure in quartersawn white oak.

SPECIFICATIONS

- DIMENSIONS
  84 in. long, 37 in. deep, and 29 in. high.

- MATERIALS
  Quartersawn white oak with maple seat frame and Scalamandre fabric.

- FINISH
  Oil-based stain, thinned and wiped polyurethane, and wax.

A question in the Winter 1994 issue of *Home Furniture* about how to achieve a quarter-sawn look on all four sides of an Arts and Crafts leg elicited a response that was different from my approach.

The posts for my "Stickley Prairie Settle" were capped by the shelf on top, so I did not have to worry about having a solid core. I simply mitered four quartersawn pieces together, leaving a small square opening down the center. To avoid wasting stock, I picked boards with good figure on both faces, and I nested the mitered pieces. I cut the miters on a table saw with the blade tilting toward the fence. After the initial 45° cut was made on each board, I set the rip fence to give the proper width. Then I ran the boards through, flipping them end for end each time. The feathered edges resulting from the miter cut are fragile at this point but blend together nicely during glue-up. I used a good, clean blade and was able to glue-up right off the saw.

I glued all four pieces for the post at once, using very strong, clear packing tape. I started by taping two adjacent pieces together across their outside faces in a number of places, making sure the tape was rubbed down well. Then I ran a piece of tape down the length of the joint and added the third and fourth sections in the same manner.

At both ends of the pieces, I ran one piece of tape across the faces of all four sections, leaving some extra tape at the end so that I could close the joint when I folded it together. I turned the whole thing over so that the outside faces were down and spread glue on all eight miters using a mini paint roller.

I folded the sections to make the square post and used the extra tape length at both ends to keep it closed. Then, starting at one end, I closed the joints by wrapping around and around, over-lapping the tape each time and pulling it taut. The tape must be strong enough that it will not break. It works well having two people for this part, one to pull and wrap the tape around, and the other to hold and then turn the post. If the miters were cut well, the tape will close the joints beautifully. The pressure of the tape being wrapped around the feathered edges results in corners that are already slightly rounded over.

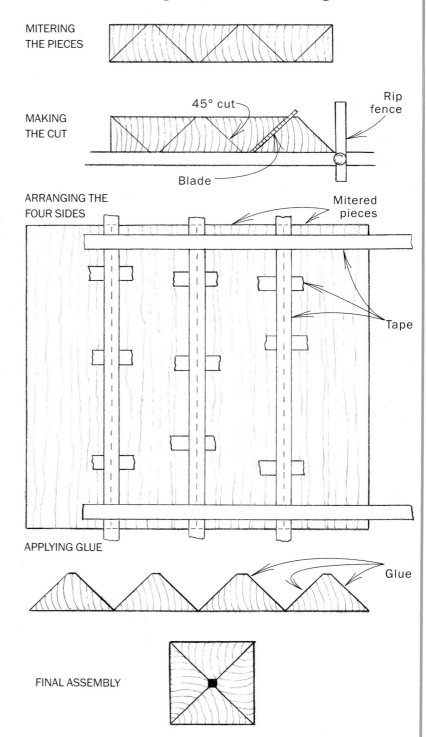

■ Making a Quartersawn Leg

MITERING THE PIECES

MAKING THE CUT

45° cut

Rip fence

Blade

ARRANGING THE FOUR SIDES

Mitered pieces

Tape

APPLYING GLUE

Glue

FINAL ASSEMBLY

MATTHEW KIRBY

Cabinet for a Wall

W hen I began designing dining-room furnishings and trimwork for some friends who were finishing a house in eastern Kansas, I fretted over just what style would be appropriate. Quite frankly, this house was designed by its owner to emphasize efficient energy use and traffic flow rather than stylistic concerns.

I thought about the design of the house and how it emerges from a gentle hillside with long, horizontal lines and low, wide overhangs. The structure looks like a Frank Lloyd Wright Prairie house. I began to pore

TRANSLATING ARTS AND CRAFTS-STYLE LINES INTO A WALL-HUNG CABINET. The author combined clean lines with straightforward joinery for an elegantly practical cabinet. Handmade ebony pulls highlight surrounding woods.

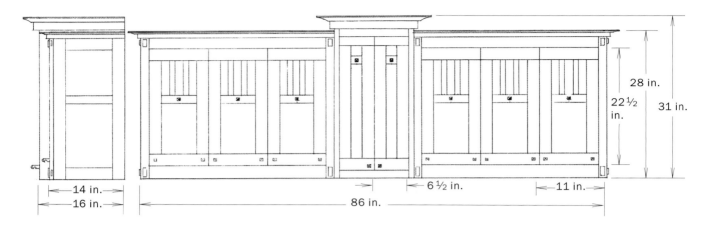

VIEW FROM TOP

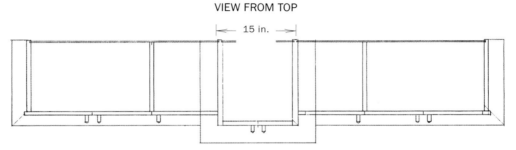

over books on Wright, Gustav Stickley, the Greene brothers and the Craftsman period. This wall-hung cabinet became much like the upper part of a hutch, with the lower part modeled after the dining-room server in a 1907 Greene brothers' house.

The center cabinet is deep enough to stack plates on shelves and to place two tall Wright candlesticks in front of the shelves. The doors ride on cup hinges, and the pulls are handmade from ebony. The hard squareness of the ebony ornaments balances the random black streaks of the spalted-maple door panels.

To me, cherry is a wood that is both majestic and very democratic. It's perfectly in sync with Stickley's writings about the Craftsman ideal, so I used cherry for the main carcase and the book-matched end panels, stiles and rails. The crown molding is coved on the table saw, and it is based on a 1910 mantel clock designed for Stickley.

A TABLE-SAW JIG FOR CUTTING COVES

The hanging wall cabinet I designed is reminiscent of the Prairie school of architecture and the work of Frank Lloyd Wright. One element that gives the cabinet that feel is the broad crown molding. I cut the cove on my table saw using an adjustable jig.

The design for this eminently simple jig grew out of a system I had devised for attaching featherboards to my table saw. The jig consists of a board with a ½-in. wide slot cut down the middle. This fence is held tight against the table by two ⅜-in. bolts that grip the T-slots milled in the top of my table saw (drawing on the facing page). The jig makes it easy to adjust the angle at which stock is cut, and the bolts ensure that the jig won't move during cutting. If your table has square slots instead of T-slots, you could attach the jig with the same kind of expanding plugs that hold down featherboards. Or you could make your own expansion plugs from wood or aluminum stock that is split so that it widens as a screw is inserted.

Coves are created by running stock over the saw blade at an angle. A cross section of a cylinder at an angle greater or lesser than perpendicular to the vertical axis will appear as an oval. This means that if you run the stock perpendicular to the blade (or parallel to the shaft), you will get a section of a circle. At an angle, out of parallel with the shaft, the section will be oval. The shape of the cove can be varied by adjusting this angle. You can use different-size blades to put a tighter curve in a smaller area.

SPECIFICATIONS

- DIMENSIONS
  16 in. deep, 31 in. tall, and 86 in. wide.

- MATERIALS
  Cherry, spalted maple, walnut, and ebony.

- FINISH
  Oil and wax.

CROWN MOLDING COVED ON A TABLE SAW. The shallow coving and the large over-hangs of crown molding for the cabinet help give it the Prairie-house look the author intended.

An Adjustable Fence for Cutting Coves

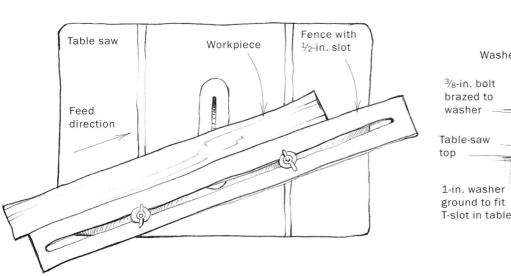

Table saw

Workpiece

Fence with ½-in. slot

Feed direction

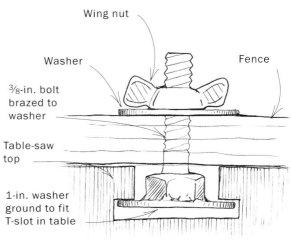

Wing nut

Washer

Fence

3/8-in. bolt brazed to washer

Table-saw top

1-in. washer ground to fit T-slot in table

GARY J. W. SPYKMAN

Marble Top Accents Oak Sideboard

SMALL OVERHANGS DIDN'T LOOK RIGHT on this piece, so the maker took a page from Prairie-style architecture and made the overhangs big.

This sideboard, which also would serve quite well as a hall table, was originally made for consignment in a gallery featuring decorative arts and furniture. But my wife insisted that we keep it. So now it stands in our living room, below a quartersawn oak wall cabinet I made for her.

Quartersawn white oak, the dominant wood of the Arts and Crafts movement, was the obvious choice for this piece. The secondary wood is ash, used for the drawer guides and the drawer sides. The

pulls are made by Acorn Manufacturing (457 School St., Mansfield, MA 02048; 800-835-0121).

I added a bottom shelf because the sideboard would have looked top-heavy without it. The shelf also is functional, providing storage for table settings, books, bowls or other decorative items.

To offset the rectilinear look of the sideboard, I added distinct profiles to the skirtboard and the backsplash. The slightly rounded profile on the skirtboard was inspired by the designs of Harvey Ellis, who had worked for Gustav Stickley. Ellis revolutionized the Arts and Crafts style by adding flowing, natural curves to his furniture.

The backsplash design is a detail used in Arts and Crafts architecture, especially in exterior trim over windows. What looks like

SPECIFICATIONS

■ DIMENSIONS
47 in. long, 18 in. wide, and 36 in. high.

■ MATERIALS
Quartersawn white oak, ash, ebony, and Balkan gray marble.

■ FINISH
Ammonia fuming, linseed oil and beeswax.

a curve is actually two lines that intersect in the center, with a slightly rounded peak.

The top of the sideboard is made of a wonderful marble called Balkan gray. Although it's not an authentic Arts and Crafts motif, the use of marble is in keeping with the spirit behind the furniture of that period. Natural materials, such as tile and leather, often were integrated into furniture designs. The marble top looks good and makes the sideboard unique. The top was made to my specifications by Rob Cimeno, a local marble and granite fabricator.

QUARTERSAWN OAK MARRIED TO MARBLE. This sideboard combines the traditional quartersawn white oak of the Arts and Crafts style with a gleaming Balkan gray marble top.

STRAIGHTFORWARD JOINERY MAKES SIDEBOARD STURDY. From the dovetailed drawers to the tenons pinned with ebony, this sideboard is built to last. Machine-cut dovetails were an Arts and Crafts standard.

KEVIN P. RODEL

Cherry Sideboard with American and British Bloodlines

INLAID SQUARES CREATE LATERAL SWEEP. The author tinkered with the inlaid squares, the overhang of the top, the width and inlay of the lower rails and the arrangement of stretchers to mitigate the strong vertical lines of the legs, the doors and the center divider.

The house was a wonderful blend of Wright-influenced Prairie-style and Shingle-style architecture built on the coast of Maine. The owners wanted a sideboard to stand in the large combined living and dining room with its stone hearth, cathedral ceiling and impressive woodwork that evoked the Craftsman era. They asked that the sideboard be tied to the overall design of the interior and that it match the cherry dining table I'd made them several years earlier. They also gave me overall dimensions I shouldn't exceed and asked that the sideboard have doors and a silverware drawer hidden behind the doors.

With this information in hand, I sat down to sketch some ideas. My overall mood for the piece would be of the Arts and Crafts period. Besides being the most appropriate for the house, it happens to be my preferred style.

A quick drawing using the given dimensions and storage requirements revealed that two pairs of doors would be most practical. My sketch was technically correct but boring. And it was too strong in its vertical lines. I prefer my designs to show an interplay of horizontal and vertical elements, with the horizontal being dominant. So I sought to make the sideboard interesting and to emphasize the horizontal.

First, I sketched a broadly overhanging top. I borrowed the curved-under shape at the edge from a piece designed by the English Arts and Crafts architect C. F. A. Voysey.

Another horizontal element, the long, broad stretcher between the sideboard's legs, with its four-square motif, adds interest and visual balance. This stretcher is filched from a table by another turn-of-the-century designer, Scotsman Charles Rennie Mackintosh.

My next revision was to widen the rail below the doors and add a simple inlay. This provides another strong horizontal element and links the sideboard to the dining table, which has a maple string inlay along its skirt.

Still, I felt there was too much vertical emphasis in the piece because of the lines of the doors and the center divider, which I'd left wide so that it relates to the center stiles on the ends of the cabinet. Then I sketched in the series of flush-inlaid maple squares, situated in line with the upper squares of the door pulls. They add a fourth horizontal element that, to my eye, balances all the features of the sideboard.

SPECIFICATIONS

■ DIMENSIONS
70 in. long, 46 in. high, and 22 in. deep.

■ MATERIALS
Cherry with maple inlay.

■ FINISH
Penetrating oil, wax.

PERIOD PULLS CINCH AN ALREADY TIGHT DESIGN. The motif of four squares in the pulls, picked up in the long stretcher, also determined the size and location of the inlaid maple squares.

ROBERT E. BROWN

Tall-Boy Chest

As a boy, I admired the chest of drawers in which my father kept his clothes and knickknacks. The "tall boy," as he called it, was simple in design and very practical. It held everything from the bulkiest sweaters to the most delicate hand-kerchiefs. It was truly a functional piece.

After a motivating trip to the Gamble House, a turn-of-the-century Craftsman style home in Pasadena, California, designed by Charles and Henry Greene, I decided to create my own tall boy. Practicality is the main focus. While the Greene brothers'

work and an oriental Craftsman style were the main design influences, the basic pro-portions of the piece are more akin to those of a toolbox belonging to a grip, an electrician or a rigger on a movie stage. Because I'm a set builder in the film indus-try, I've seen many grip's toolboxes, and I admire their shape and construction. These toolboxes are on wheels and have lots of custom-designed drawers to accommodate the tools and supplies.

In my tall boy, the irregularly sized drawers are designed to overlap like a brick

IRREGULARLY SPACED DRAWERS. Not all drawers are symmetrical to the chest's centerline (above). They are stacked like bricks in a wall, a feature of some Craftsman furniture.

A MIX OF INFLUENCES.
Childhood memories of a tall
chest belonging to the maker's
father plus a timely visit to a
famous Craftsman-era house
helped create this design.

**DETAILS ENLIVEN A RECTI-
LINEAR CASE.** A dovetailed
base (above) with a cloud-lift
motif on the front of the chest,
base molding and decorative
square pegs all add visual
interest to an otherwise
unadorned case.

wall. The cloud-lift details on the base and
the decorative square plugs on the face
frame are inspired by the Greene brothers'
designs. The red color of the piece suggests
the lacquer finishes on Chinese furniture.

I used simple techniques (glue and
nails) to build the case. The base is hand-
dovetailed. The brass drawer pulls I used
were originally far too shiny and new for
this antique-like case, so I fumed them in
ammonia for a soft patina and then rubbed
them out with 4/0 steel wool to create wear
spots that blend in with the overall look of
the cabinet.

SPECIFICATIONS

■ DIMENSIONS
49¾ in. wide, 24 in. deep, and 63 in.
high.

■ MATERIALS
Birch carcase, pine face frame, and
drawer fronts.

■ FINISH
Minwax stain and polyurethane topcoat.

RICHARD LeBLANC

Updated Mission Hall Table

In spite of all its emphasis on exposed joinery and handwork, most Mission furniture was made in production. I make my furniture in series too, and I've found that working in the Mission style is congenial to production work for a variety of reasons.

Linearity is one of the hallmarks of Mission furniture. I happen to like the linear style for aesthetic reasons, but it is also excellent for its adaptability. Working in a linear vocabulary, I can design a piece and then easily customize it, changing its length, width, or height for any number of customers without changing the essential feeling of the piece.

I also like Mission for its strength and simplicity. Take a good piece of original Mission furniture and you can drop it off a roof and only have to repair the finish. I ship furniture all over the country, so furniture built to stay together under stress appeals to me. And it is straightforward to make, so a solid piece of furniture can be produced for a reasonable price.

Although I admire Mission furniture and draw on it freely for inspiration, I'm not interested in doing reproductions. Instead, I try to design furniture that feels modern, but also seems grounded in history. I'd like to attract customers who wouldn't necessarily be interested in buying antiques. With this table, I did several things to achieve separation from the originals.

First, I avoided oak. Instead, I used burgundy-stained mahogany with a smooth

SATISFYING BUT NOT STRUCTURAL. Short corbels below the solid-lipped plywood top and faux through-tenons give this table the texture of a Morris chair.

SPECIFICATIONS

■ DIMENSIONS
48 in. long, 18 in. wide, and 30 in. high.

■ MATERIALS
Mahogany, mahogany veneer plywood and ebonized mahogany.

■ FINISH
Aniline dye, wiping stain and catalyzed lacquer.

MISSION IN TRANSITION. A bright stain finish and ebonized pulls impart a modern air to a table with the rigid lines and exposed-joinery detailing of Mission furniture.

finish to give the piece a less rustic feeling. In seeking a lighter overall appearance, I dimensioned parts on the thin side and left open spaces on either side of the spindles. And for the drawers I adapted an original pull to create a handle—a scoop in the drawer front covered with an ebonized mahogany crosspiece—that I hoped would give the table a personality of its own.

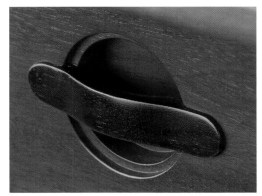

PERMANENT LOAN. LeBlanc saw a hammered-copper pull on an original Stickley piece and borrowed the design, reworking it with jazzy curves and colors (left).

SCOTT SCHMIDT

Wenge Trestle Table

BLACK BOARDS, PURE FORM. In a house full of modern art, the wenge dining table speaks with its deep color, elemental form and rough surfaces.

The rough surfaces that give this table its character came right out of working the wood. Wenge can be brittle, it splinters easily, and with its alternating hard and soft grain, it works something like aluminum laminated to balsa wood. It often tears when it's cut, and I did the rough-cutting on an ailing bandsaw that vibrated to the point of roaming around the shop. I hated the bandsaw, but I loved the sheared, torn surface the herky-jerky cutting produced. And I found that by holding the workpiece off the table a bit, I could obtain an even more sculptural surface. A similar effect could be achieved on a stable bandsaw by putting a very slight kink in a blade with a pair of pliers and by backing off the blade guides a bit, if necessary.

The rough edge looked particularly good when the adjacent surfaces were smooth and burnished. Here was a detail that expressed the wenge paradox: This wood looks placid and feels wonderfully smooth when it's finished, but it's a rascal to work.

I knew the table would need to live well in a room where there was a large, dark marble fireplace, wood floors and a wonderfully eclectic collection of artwork. There were also children and parties and any number of informal gatherings to be considered, so the table would have to be unafraid of use and expandable to accommodate 10 or 12 diners.

I sought something of the strong lines and architectural quality of the Craftsman style in my design. After the sturdy, straightforward trestle shape was set, the biggest question was material. My customers and I decided to find a dark wood with pronounced grain. I had been doing quite a bit of work in wenge at the time and was painfully aware of its working characteristics. We chose it, nevertheless, for its beautiful color, for the graphic effects of its grain, for its durability and for its gleaming smoothness in use.

I wanted to take advantage of flat-sawn wenge's attractive steely brown and black figure, so I ran the tabletop's grain lengthwise and cut the leaves at each end from the same boards as the top. To support the

ROUGH ME UP. Wenge is smooth when finished but tough to work. The table expresses that contrast, pairing smooth surfaces with rough-cut ones.

LIKE AN OLD PAIR OF JEANS.
The table's leaves fit snugly
in the strong, silky-sliding
extension arms the author
designed.

SPECIFICATIONS

■ DIMENSIONS
  72 in. long, 38 in. wide, and 29¾ in. high;
  leaves, 38 in. by 14 in.

■ MATERIALS
  Wenge.

■ FINISH
  Marine penetrating oil-and-varnish.

leaves without introducing a lot of massive
hardware, I designed a system of slotted
extension arms that accept battens screwed
to the underside of the leaves (for details
on this arrangement, see the box on the
facing page). When the leaves are in place,
the wenge's dark but definite grain is con-
tinuous from one end of the table to
the other.

CUSTOM SLIDES FOR AN EXTENDING TABLE

A dining table's leaves come out of hiding when the whole family gathers, so there's a bit of ritual around the act of putting them in place. Unfortunately, the act is often an ugly one, with people tugging in vain at opposite ends of a table, diving to hold up a suddenly unsupported expanse of mahogany, or groping for hidden cam locks. I wanted to make the act of adding a leaf to be a pleasure, so I designed an extension system for my "Wenge Trestle Table."

To avoid all the problems of a table that splits in the center, I decided to add a leaf at both ends. I arrived at the idea of having a pair of cleats screwed to the underside of each leaf. Each cleat would fit snugly into a slotted sliding apron. I had been working with extruded metal U-channel on another project, and it occurred to me that I could make the same shape in wood and achieve the strength and rigidity this job demanded. I made a long, T-sectioned hanger, which is screwed and glued to the underside of the table, and a mating slide with a T-shaped channel. When the slide is pulled out, the leaf's cleat drops right into it. I fitted the slide with a stop and an end block, both very carefully positioned, so the leaf is a pleasingly snug fit.

I made adjustable stops to limit the travel of the aprons. Each stop had a block screwed and glued to the underside of the table, and a disk of Baltic birch screwed to the apron. I put the screw through the disk off-center, so it acts as a cam to permit fine-tuning. I glued leather to the block where the disk made contact.

I made all the visible parts of the mechanism of wenge. However, for the crossbar of the T, a thin piece that must glide smoothly and take a lot of stress, I used Delrin, a tough, slippery plastic akin to Teflon but very dense. I've also used phenolic in this application, but Delrin is easy to plane, drill, saw and even joint with woodworking tools. I used tension washers, which are slightly cone shaped, to make certain the hanger screws would stay tight.

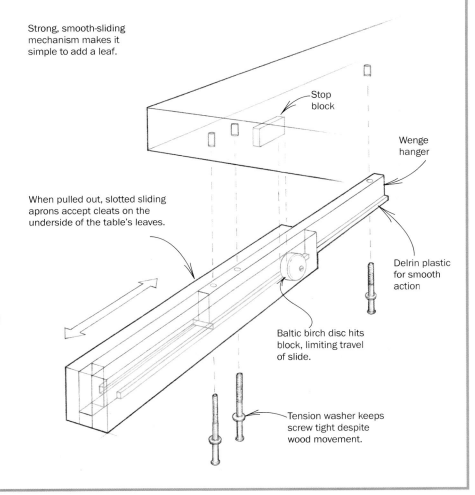

Strong, smooth-sliding mechanism makes it simple to add a leaf.

Stop block

Wenge hanger

When pulled out, slotted sliding aprons accept cleats on the underside of the table's leaves.

Delrin plastic for smooth action

Baltic birch disc hits block, limiting travel of slide.

Tension washer keeps screw tight despite wood movement.

RICH PREISS

A Craftsman's Bed

CRAFTSMAN CONTEMPO-RIZED. Using a familiar motif as a springboard, the author created this modern interpretation of the Craftsman style in untraditional bubinga and walnut.

Tradition is not only an inspiration, it is a resource. Tradition, after all, either renews itself or it dies. But despite all the affection shown towards a particular style of furniture, there is often a disdain for modern interpretations, regardless of the quality. Pondering this dilemma, I returned from an Arts and Crafts conference last year determined to make a contemporary object that might charm, if not change, even the most conservative attitude.

My intent was not to reproduce the Craftsman style but to add to what already existed. I wanted to make something whose proportions and construction methods captured the ethos of the period without being slave to its limitations. Given that queen-size beds were unknown at the turn of the century, my bed could not be a period piece. Furthermore, I had a different palette in mind. The surfaces of quartersawn oak were a product of a particular time. I wanted to exploit a contrast between slats and frame with walnut and bubinga.

To prepare for this project, I reviewed my books and notes on Craftsman furniture. I placed my lumber on two sawhorses and studied it. Quickly and disappointingly it became apparent that there was not enough material to use solid bubinga for the entire frame. Rather than resorting to a phone search for more wood, I decided to saw certain planks into veneers for each crosspiece in which the end grain would not show. I laid out each surface with all the care that I could muster, letting the grain follow the shape wherever possible.

One hundred and seventy-six mortises and tenons later, the bed was almost done. To my eye, the grain figure and reddish-purple hue of the bubinga stands midway between the brown tones of Stickley and the decorative designs of Charles and Henry Greene. The walnut spindles, reflecting my interest in contrasts within darker

SIMILAR DETAILS ON A DIFFERENT PALETTE. The slats and corbels are drawn from Gustav Stickley, but the contrasting colors in this rendition veer from the customary quartersawn oak of Craftsman furniture.

SPECIFICATIONS

■ DIMENSIONS
87½ in. long, 73½ in. wide, 50½ in. high (headboard), and 32 in. high (footboard).

■ MATERIALS
Bubinga and walnut.

■ FINISH
Synthetic oil-based varnish.

tonal ranges, add a different kind of figure as well.

The finished piece is a pleasing and much needed addition to our bedroom. Its roots in historic design bring tradition to our lives, a reminder of the values of craft, hearth and home that are part of the Craftsman legacy. Making the bed, for me, brought life to the tradition.

REX ALEXANDER builds furniture and cabinetry in Brethren, Michigan.

ROBERT E. BROWN is originally from London and now lives in Glendale, California, where he builds sets for movies and television commercials. His furniture shows influences of the Arts and Crafts era. (RobBrownFurniture@yahoo.com; 818-409-0952)

ANNETTE CARRUTHERS teaches Art History and Museum and Gallery studies at the University of St. Andrews in Scotland. She is co-author of two books on the Arts and Crafts collections at Cheltenham Art Gallery & Museum: *Simplicity or Splendour,* and *Good Citizen's Furniture.*

B. A. HARRINGTON is a 1994 graduate of the Cabinet and Furniture Making Program at the North Bennet Street School in Boston, Massachusetts. She maintains a furniture studio, where she works on one-of-a-kind commissions and speculative pieces. Her speculative work combines her background as a feltmaker with her more recently acquired woodworking skills.

IAN INGERSOLL designs and builds furniture in West Cornwall, Connecticut.

ERIC KEIL designs and builds custom furniture in Wilkes-Barre, Pennsylvania.

MATTHEW KIRBY does design-build work and sculpture, much of which is in the Arts and Crafts style. He is currently producing sculptural and architectural elements for the National D-Day Memorial in Bedford, Virginia.

STEPHEN LAMONT is a craftsman-tutor at the Edward Barnsley Educational Trust in Hampshire, England.

RICHARD LeBLANC currently works with architects, designers, home builders and woodworkers in the selection and use of wood veneers. He lives in Seattle, Washington.

BARBARA MAYER writes about furniture history and design and is the author of *In the Arts and Crafts Style* (Chronicle Books, 1992).

JOHN McALEVEY teaches at the Center for Furniture Craftsmanship in Rockport, Maine, and builds one-of-a-kind furniture in a shop next to his home in Tenants Harbor.

LARS MIKKELSEN is a furnituremaker in Santa Margarita, Calif.

PATRICK NELSON designs and builds furniture professionally in Fulton, Missouri. David Mount, an amateur woodworker in Two Harbors, Minnesota, assisted in the writing of his article.

RICH PREISS teaches furniture design and woodworking at the College of Architecture at the University of North Carolina at Charlotte, where he is the Director of Laboratories. A former consulting editor for Fine Woodworking magazine, he designs, writes about and builds furniture.

KEVIN P. RODEL and his wife, Susan C. Mack, design and build Arts and Crafts-inspired custom furniture in Pownal, Maine. They have been self-employed since 1985. (Mack & Rodel Studio, 44 Leighton Rd., Pownal, ME 04069; 207-688-4483; www.neaguild.com/macrodel)

MARIO RODRIGUEZ is a consultant to Lie-Nielsen Toolworks. He is also a teacher and the author of *Traditional Woodwork*, as well as a contributing editor for *Fine Woodworking*.

GARY ROGOWSKI designs and builds furniture in Portland, Oregon, and runs his own school there, The Northwest Woodworking Studio. He was awarded a fellowship for his design work, which has been shown in galleries nationwide. Gary is also a contributing editor for *Fine Woodworking*.

SCOTT SCHMIDT has been making custom furniture for twenty years. After attending art school, he restored Colonial houses and began making furniture (The Button Factory, 855 Islington St., Portsmouth, NH 03801; 603-436-6555).

DAVE SIGMAN built a couple of snazzy treehouses as a kid and has been hooked on woodworking ever since. He makes custom cabinets and doors in his one-man shop (43751 Little Lake Rd., Mendocino, CA 95460; 707-937-4680).

GARY J. W. SPYKMAN specializes in building hand-made furniture, fine cabinetry and custom architectural interiors. Having recently relocated from Martha's Vineyard to New Hampshire, he and his apprentices work out of a light-filled 3,500-sq.-ft. shop, located in an old mill.

THOMAS HUGH STANGELAND is a professional furnituremaker in Seattle, Washington. He builds contemporary furniture inspired by the design language of Greene and Greene.

C. MICHAEL VOGT produces custom furniture and woodworking from his home workshop, including corporate and residential furniture, museum displays, and timber-framing. An important area of woodworking for him is reforesting and managing the woodlands on his family's rural property outside Saratoga Springs.

CREDITS

Rex Alexander (photographer): 55

Vince Babak (illustrator): 63, 106–107

Jonathan Binzen (photographer): 6–8, 12, 13, 14 (top), 15, 18, 20 (top), 23–25, 43, 46–47, 158–160

John Birchard (photographer): 142–143

Keith Brofsky (photographer): 156–157

Anatole Burkin (photographer): 54, 56 (left, bottom right), 57

Annette Carruthers (photographer): 11 (bottom)

Cheltenham Art Gallery & Museums, Gloucester/Bridgeman Art Library, London (photographs): 9 (bottom), 10

David Rago Auctions Inc. (photograph): 29 (top)

William Duckworth (photographer): 36, 38–40, 42, 102

Scott Gibson (photographer): 154–155

Dennis Griggs (photographer): 16–17 (photo taken at the University of Southern Maine Wolfe's Neck Conference House in Freeport, Maine); 19, 21, 96, 99, 103, 136 (large), 152–153

Jim Phillips Photography (photograph): 28 (furniture courtesy M. T. Maxwell Furniture Co.)

Susan Kahn (photographer): 20 (bottom)

Matthew Kirby (illustrator): 148–149

Doug Koch (photographer): 147, 149

Greg Krogstad (photographer): 22; 33 (top) (courtesy Tom Stangeland)

Peter Krumhardt (photographer): 132

Heather Lambert (illustrator): 37–39, 44

Bob LaPointe (illustrator): 49, 54, 58–59, 69, 72, 74–75, 81–82, 88–89, 91, 99–102, 110–111, 117, 120, 122, 128–129, 132–133

Vincent Laurence (photographer): 70–71, 73, 76–77, 78 (large), 79–82, 84, 90–92, 94, 95 (top, middle), 109, 112–115, 118, 120, 122–123, 133–135, 136 (inset), 137–139

Maria Meleschnig (illustrator): 24–26

The Naturalist Home Furnishings Co., Provo, Utah (photograph): 30 (top)

Lance Patterson (photographer): 144–145

Michael Pekovich (photographer): 60–62, 64–65, 67, 104–105

Randall Perry (photographer): 30 (bottom) (courtesy Cotswold Furniture Makers)

Scott Phillips (photographer): 116

Jim Piper (photographer): 68, 78 (inset), 87, 95 (bottom)

Dean Powell (photographer): 32 (bottom) (courtesy David Hellman)

David Ramsey (photographer): 162–163

Jeffrey A. Rycus (photographer): 52–53, 56 (top right)

Mark Sant'Angelo (illustrator): 161

Robert Schellhammer (photographer): 150–151

Timothy Schreiner (photographer): 125, 127 (top left)

Mark Schwartz (photographer): 31, 32 (top) (courtesy Berkeley Mills, Berkeley, Calif.)

Matt Spaulding (photographer): 29 (bottom) (courtesy Green Design Furniture Co.)

Becky Staynor (photographer): 33 (bottom) (courtesy Kevin Kopil Furniture Designs)

Matthew Teague (photographer): 107–108, 126, 127 (top right, bottom), 128, 130–131

Victoria & Albert Museum, London/Bridgeman Art Library, London (photograph): 9 (top)

Alex Waters (photographer): 48, 50–51

Woodley & Quick/Cheltenham Art Gallery & Museums (photographs): 11 (top), 14 (bottom)

METRIC EQUIVALENCE CHART

Inches	Centimeters	Millimeters	Inches	Centimeters	Millimeters
⅛	0.3	3	12	30.5	305
¼	0.6	6	13	33.0	330
⅜	1.0	10	14	35.6	356
½	1.3	13	15	38.1	381
⅝	1.6	16	16	40.6	406
¾	1.9	19	17	43.2	432
⅞	2.2	22	18	45.7	457
1	2.5	25	19	48.3	483
1¼	3.2	32	20	50.8	508
1½	3.8	38	21	53.3	533
1¾	4.4	44	22	55.9	559
2	5.1	51	23	58.4	584
2½	6.4	64	24	61.0	610
3	7.6	76	25	63.5	635
3½	8.9	89	26	66.0	660
4	10.2	102	27	68.6	686
4½	11.4	114	28	71.1	711
5	12.7	127	29	73.7	737
6	15.2	152	30	76.2	762
7	17.8	178	31	78.7	787
8	20.3	203	32	81.3	813
9	22.9	229	33	83.8	838
10	25.4	254	34	86.4	864
11	27.9	279	35	88.9	889
			36	91.4	914